THE
SUBSTANCE
of LEADERSHIP

PRAISE FOR

THE SUBSTANCE
OF LEADERSHIP

"The concepts of Culture, People, and Mission are timeless principles for leading every organization regardless of scale. *The Substance of Leadership* is a must read for every purpose-driven leader looking to build a high-performing team. Dave has nailed it through this enduring framework for success given his distinguished career of leadership and serving our country."

Carl Liebert
CEO, kwx/Keller Williams

"*The Substance of Leadership* is the most applicable and practical guide on leadership I've read in recent years. Dave Robinson provides a new lens, beyond just theory, to build your leadership style for real world effectiveness, while blending personal stories with practical examples. This is a must-read for any established or aspiring leader looking to take their leadership to the next level."

Elizabeth Lamkin, MHA
CEO & Partner, PACE Healthcare Consulting, LLC

"Having worked directly with Dave to implement a leadership program based on the framework in *The Substance of Leadership*, I know first-hand the power of Dave's advice and insights. Any leader aspiring to elevate the performance of their team or organization should have a copy of this book. I wish I had it years earlier in my career."

Adrian Gottschalk

President & CEO, Foghorn Therapeutics

"Colonel Dave Robinson, USMC (Ret) has written an exceptional 'how to' on leadership—something I believe he is eminently qualified to write about. Dave earned a sterling reputation as a fighter pilot, thinker and doer throughout his career—but it was his leadership that truly stood out to me. Thoughtful, principled, hands-on servant leadership was something Dave gave to his Marines and their families every day. It was a joy and an honor to serve alongside him. Anyone can benefit from reading this book —myself included. I enthusiastically recommend it."

Semper Fi,

Lieutenant General Jon M. Davis, USMC (Ret)

President, Green Monarchs Enterprises

Chairman of the Board of Directors, Rolls-Royce North America

"Dave Robinson's *The Substance of Leadership* is a stunning front line tour of leadership in our time. Devotedly researched and brilliantly written, it is complete, concise, and sparkling with practical examples and inspirational stories. A true handbook, it is written to do real work, living dogeared in the briefcase, carry-on, and top drawer of everyone who feels the weight and passion of being a leader today."

Ian Schillinger

Managing Vice President, Capital One

"I have known Dave Robinson almost 40 years and observed him as a Naval Academy midshipman, a Marine Corps officer, and an entrepreneur and consultant. I can state unequivocally that Dave is an exceptional leader and has practiced and demonstrated all the principles presented in this book. I am grateful he has taken the time to share his knowledge, experience, and wisdom to help others lead with character, competence, and composure. Corporate, public, non-profit, military, academic, and athletic leaders would all be well-served by reading, studying, and applying the leadership framework presented in *The Substance of Leadership*. With Dave showing the way, this practical book has the potential to transform ordinary leaders and organizations into extraordinary ones!"

Arthur J. Athens

Retired Marine and former Director of the Naval Academy's Vice Admiral Stockdale Center for Ethical Leadership

"Colonel Robinson's, *The Substance of Leadership*, stands head-and-shoulders above all the other leadership books I have read. It is a wonderfully guided experiential journey through the in-and-outs of leadership. His true-life stories will have you on the edge of your seat; his distilled wisdom speaks to everyday issues that leaders confront; and the put-into-practice-today applications will make you a front-runner. Instill his *People, Culture, Mission* approach and I promise you will develop as a better, more confident leader."

Jeff Cranston

Lead Pastor and author

"A must-read for all leaders! The timeless, transferable principles in *The Substance of Leadership* will be the foundation of your leadership journey at any stage and a reference to refer back to when you inevitably get lost from time to time. No surprise, the amazing Dave 'Cru' Robinson found a way to condense leadership into easy-to-remember principles wrapped up in riveting personal stories."

Patrick Guinee, DVM
Biotech Executive

"*The Substance of Leadership* is full of practical tools gleaned by the author from years leading in the U.S. Marine Corps' most responsible positions to his work today with some of the high-flying leaders in the wider business world. I can picture Dave Robinson here as a junior officer, entrusted with millions of dollars worth of aircraft and, even more, with the precious lives of his Marines; to Dave today, handed responsibility for the world's most complex systems and expensive equipment. At every step along the way, from a newbie pilot to an experienced source trusted by his clients, Dave keeps two things in mind: he is dealing with difficult problems and he is entrusted with the lives of the people who deal with those issues day-to-day. He breaks down his approach here brilliantly, pulling out the step-by-step processes and marrying them to an ongoing concern for the welfare of the organization."

Ed Ruggero
Business consultant, historian, motivational speaker, author of 11 books

"*The Substance of Leadership* is an authentic resource that applies to any person leading a team. Dave does an excellent job breaking down what really matters in a high performing organization. He uses his real experiences and gives examples on how you can apply them in your everyday environment. This is a must-read for anyone who is looking to grow as a leader."

Justin Harvey

President & CEO, Premier Exteriors

"One of the best leadership books I have read. Both inspiring and insightful, *The Substance of Leadership* should be required reading by every leader across every industry. Clear, concise, effective, David Robinson has written an entertaining and engaging book full of captivating personal leadership anecdotes. He's distilled over three decades of high-performance leadership experience into a blueprint for how you, regardless of position, can lead a high-performing team."

Carey D. Lohrenz

Former U.S. Navy fighter pilot, CEO, WSJ best-selling author, *Fearless Leadership: High-Performance Lessons from the Flight Deck* and *Span of Control*

THE
SUBSTANCE
of LEADERSHIP

A PRACTICAL FRAMEWORK FOR
EFFECTIVELY LEADING A HIGH-PERFORMING TEAM

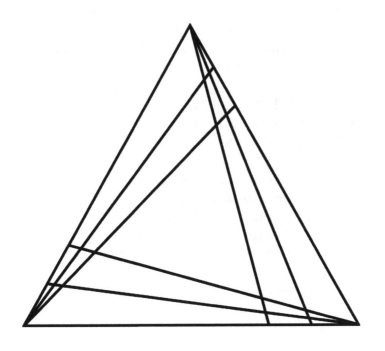

DAVID ROBINSON

Published in association with Per Capita Publishing, a division of Content Capital®.

ISBN 13: 978-1-954020-09-2 (Hardback)
ISBN 13: 978-1-954020-11-5 (Paperback)
ISBN 13: 978-1-954020-10-8 (Ebook)

Library of Congress Cataloging-in-Publication Data
Names: Robinson, David, author.
Title: The Substance of Leadership / David Robinson
Description: First Edition | Texas: Per Capita Publishing (2021)
Identifiers: LCCN 2021910893 (print)

14 15 16 17 18 19 10 9 8 7 6 5 4 3 2 1

First Edition

To all of the Marines I know who set the example,
and many who carried me on their shoulders,
thank you for teaching me how to lead.

TABLE OF CONTENTS

ABOUT THE AUTHOR

Dave Robinson is a senior executive and retired U.S. Marine Corps colonel with over three decades of experience leading complex organizations and high-performing teams. A former fighter pilot and TOPGUN instructor, Dave is an expert and international speaker on the subjects of organizational leadership and performance improvement, and a senior advisor to Fortune 1000 companies in the realm of mission-critical operations with a focus on strategy, change management, and leadership development in high-reliability industries including aerospace and defense, transportation and logistics, safety and security, construction, energy, advanced manufacturing, healthcare, and biotechnology.

Throughout his twenty-five-year military career, Dave served in several executive leadership positions in the areas of strategy, operations, logistics, maintenance, safety, communications, human resources, education, and training. He flew over 3,500 hours, 200 aircraft carrier landings, and 100 combat missions in the FA-18 Hornet, and was awarded the Bronze Star Medal for supervising over 20,000 combat missions and more than 2,000 medical evacuations while serving as the Director of Air Operations in Iraq.

Dave also served as a strategy director for the Chairman of the Joint Chiefs of Staff, where he facilitated numerous studies used to develop the Pentagon's ten-year vision and budget for the Department of Defense. In his final assignment, he was the commanding officer (CEO) of a $12 billion aviation enterprise where he managed operations, training, safety, logistics, maintenance, and sustainment for a fleet of 250 jet aircraft and led over 2,500 personnel supporting global operations.

During his time in uniform, Dave discovered that one of his passions is helping leaders succeed. In 2011 he founded Vertical Performance Enterprises to help leaders take their teams to the next level through the application of proven leadership principles and performance-improvement fundamentals that have consistently produced winning results in some of the most complex, uncertain, and dynamic environments in the world.

Dave graduated with distinction from the United States Naval Academy with a bachelor's degree in systems engineering, and subsequently earned a master's degree in national security strategy from the National Defense University in Washington, DC. He and his family live in Hilton Head, South Carolina.

INTRODUCTION

It was a dark night in the Pacific Ocean during the spring of 1993. We were in the final phase of workups for an upcoming combat deployment to the Persian Gulf aboard the aircraft carrier USS *Abraham Lincoln*—a nuclear-powered floating city with more than seventy aircraft and 5,000 people living in a multi-storied maze barely 1,000 feet long and 200 feet wide, and operating in one of the most dangerous environments in the world.

I was a rookie FA-18 pilot recently assigned to my first fighter squadron at Marine Corps Air Station El Toro near Irvine, California. Having just graduated from the U.S. Naval Academy and completed initial flight training, I only had a few dozen carrier landings, or "traps," under my belt, which was not nearly enough to feel comfortable landing aboard an aircraft carrier at night . . . especially in bad weather.

Ninety minutes earlier I had catapulted off the carrier for an air-to-air training mission. The weather wasn't great, but it was above minimum requirements, and it was forecast to stay that way through the end of our flight operations.

When it was time to return to the ship, I checked in with the *Lincoln's* air traffic control to receive my landing sequence instructions, along with the other twenty aircraft that were airborne at the time. The first thing I noticed was that the controller's voice was a bit more tense than usual. He informed me that the weather had deteriorated more rapidly than forecast and that unexpected rough seas were causing the flight deck to pitch significantly. Later I would learn that "significantly" meant up to forty-foot vertical fluctuations.

As if this wasn't enough stress already for a rookie pilot with just a few dozen traps, we were also conducting "blue water operations"—meaning there were no land-based divert fields available. If I couldn't get aboard prior to reaching emergency fuel state, I had two options: either hope I could find an airborne tanker to give me enough gas for another attempt, or plan to eject close to the ship and hope the search-and-rescue helicopter could find me among the surging waves in reduced visibility.

Landing aboard an aircraft carrier is like trying to land on your driveway at 160 miles per hour. Only imagine that your driveway is simultaneously rolling left and right, pitching up and down, and moving forward at thirty-five miles per hour. Doing this in the dark is exponentially harder, no matter how much experience you have.

Fortunately, the FA-18 has a precise heads-up display with an instrument landing system, which is extremely helpful during night carrier landings. Unfortunately, my heads-up display went blank due to a generator surge during my catapult shot ninety minutes earlier, and I wasn't able to revive it during the flight.

So as they say, "there I was"—a rookie FA-18 pilot somewhere over the Pacific Ocean, at night, in bad weather, too far from land for any divert field options, with a pitching deck like I had never seen before. Based on my fuel state, I had four attempts to get aboard.

At three quarters of a mile from the ship on my first approach, air traffic control handed me off to the landing signal officer (LSO) who was positioned as usual on the flight deck near the landing area with a radio to help talk nervous pilots like me aboard. Five seconds prior to landing the LSO told me to "wave off" due to the pitching deck. I happened to be coming down at the same time the pitching deck was coming up, and due to bad timing I was being set up for a potential "crash landing." So I selected full power on the throttles, climbed to 1,200 feet, and started a left turn as air traffic control began to sequence me back into the traffic pattern. I now had three attempts remaining.

On my second approach, everything was looking good until the LSO again told me to wave off—this time for a "foul deck." The aircraft ahead of me required a little more time than normal getting out of the wires and taxiing clear of the landing area, which posed the risk of a collision had I continued with my landing. Again, I selected full power, climbed to 1,200 feet, and started a left turn as air traffic control began to sequence me back into the traffic pattern. I now had two attempts remaining and was starting to sweat.

On my third approach, air traffic control vectored me to a good starting position and thankfully there were no wave-off calls from the LSO. However, a few seconds prior to landing I started to settle slightly below the desired 3.5-degree glideslope to the landing area. The margin of error for catching a wire is pretty slim. If you are more than five feet high, there is a good chance you will land beyond the last wire, resulting in an unintentional touch-and-go called a "bolter." If you are more than five feet low there is a near-certain chance that the LSO will tell you to wave off due to the unacceptable risk of crashing into the back edge of the flight deck.

Due to rookie nerves, I overcontrolled my settle below the glideslope by adding too much power, which caused me to bolter.

I selected full power, climbed to 1,200 feet, and started a left turn as air traffic control began to sequence me back into the traffic pattern with an emergency vector to the final approach course. I had one attempt remaining, and now I was sweating bullets.

As I was setting up for my last approach, the LSO addressed me on the radio by my call sign in a calm, reassuring voice and said, "Crusoe, we've got you. Just listen closely and do exactly what I say, and I'll get you aboard." As I began my descent to the landing area on my final attempt, fortunately I didn't receive any wave-off calls. But just like the previous attempt, I settled below glideslope again and overcontrolled my error with too much power. Instantly the LSO said, "Easy with it"—which was guidance for me to pull a little power off before climbing above the glideslope—and then he immediately followed with, "Power back on" just in time to cushion me into the wires.

It was the greatest feeling in the world when I lunged forward in my straps as my FA-18 decelerated from 160 miles per hour to a stop in less than two seconds. I quickly pulled the throttles to idle and raised my hook. After locating my taxi director, I began taxiing toward my parking spot on the forward edge of the ship as massive swells caused the flight deck to pitch up and down with an erratic rhythm while salt water from the crashing waves sprayed over the bow. Once my taxi director gave me the signal that I was properly secured to the flight deck with chocks and chains, I shut the engines down and breathed a huge sigh of relief.

I raised the canopy, exited the cockpit, and climbed down the jet's ladder to the flight deck ten feet below. As I stood there watching several other aircraft safely recover, I realized I was witnessing one of the most incredible orchestrations of teamwork that I had ever seen in my life. Five thousand people were working together as one to recover nearly two dozen aircraft in less than thirty minutes under some of the most dangerous and demanding conditions imaginable.

Ten decks below, the nuclear propulsion crew was working hard to keep the 100-ton ship steaming ahead through the surging waves. Ten stories above the flight deck, the captain and his crew were focused on navigating and steering the ship to keep thirty knots of wind straight down the runway. On the flight deck, hundreds of young men and women with an average age barely over twenty years old were recovering and parking aircraft in one-minute intervals like a perfectly synchronized orchestra as the "air boss" conducted movements from the tower above. The controllers in the carrier's air traffic control room were equally impressive as they creatively re-sequenced multiple aircraft back into the landing pattern following numerous missed approaches. And barely ten feet from the wires, the LSOs were on the radio talking nervous pilots like me safely aboard.

Two months later we deployed to the Persian Gulf for combat operations, where I witnessed that same level of teamwork day after day for six months. At that point I was determined to know, *What are the essential elements of leadership that enable this team to perform at such a consistently high level under such demanding conditions?*

I considered that question often during the next twenty years of my military career. Throughout all of my leadership experiences, two things were abundantly clear. First, leadership isn't easy. And second, while I am sure there are a handful of born leaders out there in the world somewhere, the reality is that most of us have to *learn* to lead.

When I transitioned from the military to the private sector in 2012, I was asked by a friend in a Fortune 100 company if I could speak to a group of executives on the subject of how to lead a high-performing team in a dynamic, fast-paced, high-pressure environment. I was honored that he asked, and I told him it would be a privilege to share my thoughts. But as I began to structure and outline my ideas, I soon realized how challenging the task would be. Basically, I needed to synthesize three decades of leadership lessons into a concise framework that I could explain in less than an hour to an audience of diverse leaders from a wide range of industries.

This forced me to wrestle more deeply with that original question from twenty years earlier: *What matters most with regard to leading a high-performing team in an environment of uncertainty, volatility, and pressure?* And more specifically, *How can we learn to effectively lead?*

Despite the challenge, it was one of the most rewarding tasks I've ever undertaken. It pushed me to condense three decades of observing and serving on dozens of teams into a simple framework comprised of *three* fundamental focus areas that I believe are essential to leading a high-performing team: *culture*, *people*, and *mission*.

I started this process by considering all of the leadership principles I'd been taught as a midshipman at the U.S. Naval Academy and as a junior officer in the U.S. Marine Corps. Then, referencing my personal leadership journals and files, I thought about the most effective leaders I'd ever worked for and the highest-performing teams I'd ever served on. Contrasting these examples with less effective leaders and lower-performing teams, I distilled my original list of leadership principles into those I believed were most important from a follower's perspective.

Next, I applied the lens of my own experience leading teams from dozens to thousands of people. I considered the most important lessons I had learned about how to effectively lead a high-performing team, and how not to. Many of these lessons I learned during four intensive years as the commanding officer of Marine aviation units, where ultimate accountability for mission readiness and the lives of everyone in the organization pushed my leadership to depths I'd not previously fathomed. Others I learned in combat, where the stakes were even higher. Some I learned teaching high-performing teams for three years as a TOPGUN instructor. And several of the lessons I learned the hard way.

As a commanding officer, it was my practice to thoughtfully develop and share written leadership advice with my direct reports during onboarding, which I hoped would help them succeed as leaders and prevent them from having to learn lessons the hard way. As a result of mentoring them through challenges and observing the performance of their teams in the months that followed, I was able to glean even deeper insights into the most important leadership qualities that enable high-performance teamwork.

When I reviewed these lessons from my own leadership experience, I was able to further distill my original list of leadership principles into nine key leadership qualities that fell into the three categories I previously mentioned: *culture*, *people*, and *mission*. Based on everything I've learned about leading teams in dynamic operational environments, while considering the fact that our time and energy are finite resources, I believe these are the three essential areas to focus on in order to maximize your leadership effectiveness. By doing so, you can maximize your chances of creating an environment where your people are inspired to pour their hearts into your mission and achieve their full potential as a team.

The most rewarding aspect of this process was that it enabled me to convey in a concise way how leaders can *learn* to lead a high-performing team by focusing on these three essentials. Since speaking to that first group of leaders in 2012, I've had the privilege of sharing the framework with thousands of people in dozens of audiences across a wide range of organizations and industries. Each time I share it, my hope is twofold. First, that something I say will help someone in the audience become a better leader. Second, that the life of someone who works for that leader will be enriched. I'm always encouraged and grateful I can help when afterward someone says, "Thank you for simplifying leadership into practical terms and showing me where to focus." And I'm even more moved when someone tells me, "I wish my boss could hear this." Those two comments are the impetus behind this book.

Through my consulting work in the private sector over the past decade, I've gained further insights that have helped me expand the framework in two dimensions. First, I've gained a deeper understanding of the interdependencies between the three essentials and how leaders can connect them in a synergistic way. Second, I've gained a greater appreciation for valuable ways that business leaders can apply the framework to maximize their leadership effectiveness. Both of these dimensions have been instrumental in helping me teach and coach leaders how to effectively lead a high-performing team.

If you're a leader who is struggling with where to focus your time and energy in order to maximize your leadership effectiveness, then this book is for you. Perhaps you are an experienced leader, but you feel like you are constantly putting out fires. Maybe you were recently promoted to a new leadership position, and your scope of responsibility is daunting. Or possibly you've never led a team before, but now you are. Regardless of your situation, one thing is certain. The pressure is on, and you are expected to perform. I want to help.

Leading well demands personal accountability, self-sacrifice, and self-discipline. It requires courage and perseverance. It entails tremendous time and energy. And it takes extraordinary focus. Because your plate is always overflowing. You are constantly under pressure. The problems keep coming. Uncertainty and volatility abound. People are complicated. The expectations on you are high. The burden of leadership can be heavy. And it's often a lonely job.

But I can't think of many endeavors in life where you can have more impact and make more of a difference in people's lives than the profession of leadership. Every day you have the opportunity to help individuals and teams reach their full potential. And that's why I'm excited to share this book with you.

My hope is that something I've learned in my journey might resonate with you in a way that helps you become a more effective and successful leader, so that you can create greater impact in the world and help those you lead to have a more rewarding and fulfilling life.

With this in mind, I've organized the three essential focus areas into a basic framework that we will unpack together in chapters 1–3. In chapters 4–6 we'll expand the framework and talk about how to connect these three essentials together in a synergistic way. In the final section, chapters 7–9, we'll discuss ways to apply the framework to maximize your leadership effectiveness. For easy reference, the framework's key components and many of the practical tools that we will discuss are also included in the appendix.

By the end of the book, I hope the framework we build and unpack together will help unlock a deeper understanding of three things: the essential fundamentals of leadership; how you can apply these fundamentals in a practical, focused way that will maximize your leadership effectiveness and elevate your team's performance; and how you can help the people on your team reach their full potential and find fulfillment in their work.

Thank you for coming along for the ride. If past or present leadership experiences have felt more like a fast-moving, nerve-racking carrier landing on a stormy night, I'm here to help talk you aboard. It will be the best feeling in the world when you reach your destination, take time to reflect on your team, and say to yourself, "I think I'm witnessing one of the most amazing orchestrations of teamwork I've ever seen." I hope you enjoy the journey.

SECTION I
Essentials

In this section we'll build the basic framework for leading a high-performing team. The framework is called the *leadership triad*, and is comprised of three essential focus areas: *culture*, *people*, and *mission*. In chapter 1, we'll discuss the center of gravity of a high-performing culture—*trust*, and we'll unpack three vital leadership qualities for building a culture of trust: *character*, *competence*, and *composure*. In chapter 2, we'll talk about how to focus on your *people* by *respecting*, *knowing*, and *taking care* of them in a way that inspires your team to do whatever it takes to accomplish the mission. And in chapter 3, we'll discuss three keys to *mission* focus—*prioritization*, *preparation*, and *passion* for excellence, which together will help your team reach its full potential.

CHAPTER 1

CULTURE

"Average leaders raise the bar on themselves;
good leaders raise the bar for others; great
leaders inspire others to raise their own bar."

—ORRIN WOODWARD

CULTURE

The thin orange glow along Iraq's expansive desert horizon to the west had just settled into dusk. I snapped night vision goggles onto my helmet from the back seat of the UH-60 Black Hawk helicopter as its twin engines began to whine and four rotor blades started to whirl. In the dim green lighting now emanating from the cockpit's instrument panel, I could see the two pilots meticulously cross-checking switches and gauges while they continued their start-up checklist. My seat began to gently rumble with the rest of the aircraft as the rotor blades overhead gradually reached idle rotation speed, turning the engine whine into a choppy whisper while the smell of aviation fuel wafted through the open door next to me.

I was on a "ride along" training mission with the Army medical evacuation company assigned to Al Asad air base, which is approximately 100 miles northwest of Baghdad along the Euphrates River. They were one of several aviation units integrated into our Marine aircraft wing that was deployed to Iraq in 2006. Our mission was to provide air support for 30,000 Marines and Soldiers on the ground throughout Anbar Province, which stretched from Baghdad to Iraq's western border with Syria and Jordan, and south to Saudi Arabia—an area almost twice the size of my home state of South Carolina.

I had recently reported to the aircraft wing to serve as a battle captain in the tactical air command center, where one of my responsibilities was coordinating medical evacuation (or "medevac") missions throughout our operating area. I quickly learned the importance of the "golden hour"—the narrow window of time available to get a wounded Marine or Soldier from the battlefield to a military hospital before their chance of survival dropped dramatically.

I also quickly learned how difficult this was, given the physics of time and space in an area as large as Anbar Province. So I asked the Black Hawk company commander if I could ride along on a mission to gain a better appreciation of their operating challenges, which would help me more effectively coordinate medevac missions from the command center. He agreed.

Earlier in the day, we had flown at low altitude from Al Asad to one of our perimeter operating bases near the Jordanian border for a simulated casualty drill. The pilot and copilot were seasoned warrant officers, each with over twenty years of flying experience.

The enlisted crew chief and flight medic on board each had more than a decade of experience, including multiple combat tours. While I watched the barren desert less than 100 feet below race by at 150 miles per hour, the crew was kind enough to educate me on some of the important operational requirements for a successful medevac mission, including precise command, control, and communication.

During our conversation, the pilot suddenly banked so hard to the right that I would have fallen through the open door next to me had I not been strapped to my seat. The helicopter stopped on a dime in mid-air, hovering right above a squad of Marines that I could now see directly beneath us. We briskly descended to a landing spot adjacent to the squad as the Black Hawk was enveloped in a cloud of dust. Two Marines emerged through the sandy haze—one with a simulated injury being carried by the other. Our flight medic helped the "injured" Marine onto the stretcher in front of me, and in less than thirty seconds we were lifting off.

After delivering the simulated casualty to his perimeter operating base a few minutes away, we flew forty-five minutes north toward another operating base near the Syrian border to repeat the same drill. This time when we delivered the "injured" Marine back to her base, we shut down to refuel, debrief, and grab a quick dinner in the mess tent. It was great meeting and talking with many of the men and women at the forward operating base whom I communicated with regularly from the command center. I wished we could have stayed longer, but as dusk approached, it was time to prepare for our final training mission on our way back to our home base. Aside from being a night mission, this one would be just like the previous two, or so we thought.

A fiery sunset lit up the desert sky as we walked around the Black Hawk while the crew carefully conducted pre-flight checks for our forty-minute flight back to Al Asad. The orange glow on the horizon becoming thinner was always a welcome sign that the scorching daily temperature would soon begin to cool. It was also an unwelcome reminder that the fighting would soon heat up as Al-Qaeda insurgents went to work under the cool cover of darkness.

The pilots finished their start-up checklist and began preparing for takeoff to the east. By now it was so dark that if not for the subtle green glow from the cockpit, I wouldn't have been able to see my hand in front of my face. I flipped my night vision goggles down in front of my eyes, turning the dark night into a pixelated green twilight. As the pilot increased power to the engines, the whispering rotor blades began humming and my rumbling seat settled into a steady vibration. Seconds later we elevated to 100 feet and accelerated eastward.

A few minutes later we received a call from the tactical air command center that a Marine squad on patrol was pinned down in a firefight, and one of the Marines was wounded. We were the closest medevac aircraft in the vicinity, and the golden hour clock was ticking. The copilot punched the location of the firefight into the Black Hawk's navigation system, which indicated we were twenty minutes away. Our night medevac training mission had just become real.

When we got closer to the fight, the copilot established radio contact with the senior Marine on the ground, who indicated our intended landing zone was still hot due to small arms fire. Fortunately, two AH-1 Cobra gunship helicopters had just arrived. Our copilot coordinated with the Cobra flight lead to establish a screen to suppress the insurgent fire so the Black Hawk could get in to pick up the wounded Marine and get out safely.

Once the zone was temporarily subdued, the Black Hawk pilot calmly relayed, "Medevac inbound" over the radio while skimming the terrain less than twenty feet off the ground at more than 100 miles per hour in pure darkness. Spotting the infrared strobe next to the wounded Marine through his night vision goggles, the pilot did that "stop on a dime in mid-air" thing again, then set the bird down on uneven, rocky terrain right next to the wounded Marine while the rotor blades continued to whirl. Thirty seconds later, the Marine was on board and we were racing toward the military hospital at Al Asad while the flight medic treated him for shrapnel wounds to his lower extremities.

We landed next to the hospital right at the end of the golden hour. A Navy corpsman and nurse were waiting with a stretcher to rush the wounded Marine into surgery. I said a prayer as we taxied back to the flight line. Once we were parked, the pilot shut down the aircraft, the rotor blades wound to a stop, and the engines subsided to a dull whine. When the Black Hawk was completely silent and still, we exited the aircraft, did a quick walk-around to ensure there was no battle damage, then headed inside to debrief, where we learned the Marine was in stable condition.

My emotions were all over the map: relief that the Marine would live; adrenaline-inspired exhilaration from the mission I'd just experienced; sadness for the casualties of war; pride in the team I was privileged to be a part of; respect for the Black Hawk crew's extraordinary competence and commitment; admiration for their exemplary courage and composure under pressure; appreciation for the enormous risks they were taking and sacrifices they were making to save dozens of lives each day; and immense gratitude that I could be there to witness it all.

Before I left, I thanked the crew for the opportunity to ride along and expressed my genuine admiration and appreciation for who they were and what they did every day. I'll never forget the pilot's response: "Colonel, this is our job and that's what we do. Just like your Marines trust us to be there when they need us, we trust them to get us in and out safely. It's a team effort." As I walked away, I realized I had just learned an amazing lesson about the culture of a high-performing team.

How Would *You* Describe the Culture in *Your* Organization?

Culture is the first essential focus area for leading a high-performing team, because it forms the lens through which your team members view each other and your team's mission. If you get it right, your people will do extraordinary things for each other to accomplish your mission, because they trust each other and don't want to let their team down.

Merriam-Webster defines *culture* as "the set of shared attitudes, values, goals, and practices that characterizes an institution or organization." That definition resonates with me because it describes how the mindsets of your team members intersect with their behaviors to define the essence of who your team is.

> The quality of a team's culture can be measured by the content of its character, the caliber of its competence, and the capacity of its composure.

I've found that the quality of a team's culture can be measured by the content of its character, the caliber of its competence, and the capacity of its composure under pressure. We'll talk more about each of these three areas shortly, but in the meantime, how would you describe the culture in your organization? Take a minute to think about it, because how you think about culture is critical to your success as a leader.

If you asked me how I would describe the culture on board the USS *Abraham Lincoln* that enabled the crew to perform at such a consistently high level, or in our aircraft wing in Iraq that fostered such selfless and courageous teamwork, or in every other high-performing team I've been privileged to be a part of, I could summarize them in one word: *trust*. In each case, personal and professional *trust* formed the foundation for total commitment to operational excellence that resulted in everyone on the team doing everything they could do to keep from letting their teammates down.

To effectively lead a high-performing team, the first question you should ask yourself is, "How can I create a culture of *trust?*" This is the key question that we'll unpack together in this chapter. In my experience, the answer can be found in what I call "the three C's" of a high-performing culture: *character, competence,* and *composure.* These three leadership qualities will define the quality of your culture. In other words, the quality of your culture starts with you.

> The quality of your culture starts with you.

Character Builds a Culture of Trust

The first culture-defining leadership quality is *character.* I believe the most important characteristic of character is integrity. Over the years, I've always translated integrity to members of my team simply as *doing the right thing.* Integrity is particularly critical because it's the foundation of trust—and in my experience, trust is the glue that holds a high-performing team together, especially under pressure.

Doing the Right Thing

I've seen teams unravel under pressure because they didn't trust each other. In most cases they were newly formed teams who didn't know each other very well (we'll talk about the importance of knowing your people in the next chapter), and they didn't have a strong cultural foundation to fall back on.

I experienced this personally at the beginning of my "plebe" (freshman) year at Annapolis, which is a pressure cooker by design. I was one of four new plebes in a squad with eight upperclassmen and -women who were responsible for orienting us to Navy and Marine Corps culture, and training us to perform under pressure.

> Trust is the glue that holds a high-performing team together, especially under pressure.

One of the seniors in our squad was a soon-to-be Marine lieutenant who grew up near Newark, New Jersey, and was a Naval Academy brigade boxing champion. Terry Walton (otherwise known as "Mr. Walton" or "Sir" to us plebes) looked remarkably like Louis Gossett Jr., who played the Oscar-winning role of drill instructor Emil Foley in the 1982 film *An Officer and a Gentleman*.[1] To an eighteen-year-old college freshman, he was one of the most intimidating people I'd ever met.

Mr. Walton definitely knew how to turn up the heat for the four plebes in our squad. He was a master at being in our face, screaming just the right remarks to throw us off our game while we stood at attention delivering "chow calls" involving long lists of information that we had to memorize and reel off from an assigned station before each meal. When we slipped up or froze up, he turned up the heat even louder.

To make matters worse, our squad was assigned the most centrally located and most visible chow call station possible—right in the middle of the main passageway in the area of our dormitory where the remaining 120 midshipmen in our company formed up prior to each meal. Mr. Walton seemed to relish the added visibility and additional pressure it created for the four plebes in his squad who rotated through this assignment to ensure our station was covered by one of us for every meal.

In addition to chow calls, Mr. Walton and the other upperclassmen and -women in our squad ensured that pressure permeated every aspect of our daily lives. I'm embarrassed to admit it, but the four of us slowly started trying to avoid the heat by avoiding each other. We were a newly formed team in a completely new culture, and we unfortunately succumbed to what is sometimes referred to as the "first law of thermodynamics: when the heat is on someone else, it's not on you." We started to unravel as a team. But Mr. Walton saw right through us and turned up the heat even more.

Somehow we eventually began to understand that he was actually trying to teach us an important cultural lesson: that the best way to handle the pressure individually was to work together and take the heat for each other. Then one day Mr. Walton stopped one of the other plebes in our squad who was running to our chow call station for his turn in the spotlight. Realizing that he would undoubtedly take heat for being missing in action, the remaining three of us hustled out of our respective rooms and converged at the station to cover for our teammate.

I noticed Mr. Walton watching this unfold from just down the hallway. As he strutted toward us, we braced for impact. But he didn't say a word. It was the first time I'd ever seen him smile. Terry Walton knew a thing or two about how doing the right thing builds trust and team culture. Although we still had a lot to learn and a long way to go, we were finally starting to gel.

Despite experiencing and witnessing a few other teams in my career like that one which regrettably unraveled due to undeveloped trust, fortunately I've seen far more teams stick together and thrive under pressure because they *did* trust each other. The level of trust on many of these teams was so high that team members were willing to make extraordinary personal sacrifices to help their team and do the right thing because they didn't want to let their teammates down, just like the medevac crew in Iraq.

Character Enables Your Team to Trust Your Intentions

Doing the right thing usually requires courage and discipline, because decisions frequently boil down to choosing one of two basic paths: there's the right way and then there's the wrong way. While maybe it doesn't feel so black and white, even when the choice seems like more of a gray area, you usually know in your gut what's the right thing to do.

> We violate our integrity when we don't "walk the talk," and that ultimately undermines others' trust in us.

In the realm of aviation safety, we had a saying: "If there's any doubt, there is no doubt," meaning if there is any doubt about whether or not something you are about to do is safe, then don't do it. I can confidently say I'm alive today because I lived by that rule when planning and executing every flight. I think it's also a good rule to live by as a leader in order to keep your character alive. If there's any doubt about whether or not something you are about to do is right, then follow your gut and don't do it.

The Latin root word for *integrity* means "whole" or "complete." If we know in our mind and gut what's the right thing to do but don't do it, then we divide our actions from our conscience and are no longer "whole." We violate our integrity when we don't "walk the talk," and that ultimately undermines others' trust in us. It tarnishes our leadership and erodes our culture. Of course, none of us are perfect. We all make mistakes. But when we do, admitting our shortcomings and learning from them sends a powerful signal of humility and vulnerability to our team, which can actually enhance trust.

Choosing the right way over the wrong way often demands more time and effort. In my experience, this is one of the main reasons why people take shortcuts. Seldom do leaders and team members intentionally try to do the wrong thing. It's just that shortcuts are faster and easier. But I've found that there are rarely shortcuts to excellence.

There are rarely shortcuts to excellence.

When presented with a tempting shortcut, Robert Frost's closing words in "The Road Not Taken" come to mind: "Two roads diverged in a wood, and I—I took the one less traveled by, and that has made all the difference."[2] Taking the high road and doing the right thing is often the harder road that is less traveled.

Sometimes doing the right thing requires mental and physical courage, like the medevac crew displayed in Iraq. Other times it takes moral and emotional courage. The bottom line is that it takes courage to do the right thing, regardless of the consequences, even when no one is watching. It's definitely not easy, and we all come up short at times. However, by constantly striving to do the right thing and lead with integrity, you enable your team to *trust your intentions.*

I've found that many of us learn to do the right thing from someone who models integrity. Often it's a family member, friend, teacher, leader, mentor, or other influential person who inspires us with the courage and commitment to do the right thing through their actions. This raises two important questions. First, can you point to someone who has been that person for you? If so, I encourage you to call them or write a note to thank them. Second, are you that person for your team members? If you're not sure, make a commitment to become that person, starting today.

> Having the courage to do the right thing is more important than being popular.

For me, that person was my father, Robbie Robinson. He exemplified integrity. Growing up, I can remember him often saying, "Having the courage to do the right thing is more important than being popular." Those were powerful words, but the way he lived those words spoke even more loudly to me. My dad taught me the importance of having moral and emotional courage and conviction in the face of adversity.

When I was in high school he gave me a copy of Dale Wimbrow's popular poem written in 1934 titled, "The Guy in the Glass."[3] Perhaps you've seen a slightly modified version before with the title "The Man in the Glass" and the word "self" substituted for "pelf" in the first line (pelf refers to wealth). Nevertheless, many people have found inspiration over the years from Dale's words, and I still find myself referring to them often.

When you get what you want in your struggle for pelf [riches],
And the world makes you King for a day,
Then go to the mirror and look at yourself,
And see what that guy has to say.

For it isn't your Father, or Mother, or Wife,
Who [sic] judgement upon you must pass.
The feller whose verdict counts most in your life
Is the guy staring back from the glass.
He's the feller to please, never mind all the rest,
For he's with you clear up to the end,
And you've passed your most dangerous, difficult test
If the guy in the glass is your friend.

You may be like Jack Horner and "chisel" a plum,
And think you're a wonderful guy,
But the man in the glass says you're only a bum
If you can't look him straight in the eye.

You can fool the whole world down the pathway of years,
And get pats on the back as you pass,
But your final reward will be heartaches and tears
If you've cheated the guy in the glass.

Character Requires Courage in the Face of Adversity

I wish I could say I've never cheated the guy in the glass. I can say I've tried my best not to, though. It's hard to do the right thing when faced with the lure of the crowd or the headwinds of popular opinion. Sometimes it's even harder when those headwinds are coming from senior leadership within your organization.

I learned this firsthand midway through my military career. I was the executive officer of a unit comprised of both Navy and

Marine personnel at a base in the western United States, where we reported operationally to a Navy admiral. In addition to being the executive officer, I was also the senior Marine, which meant I was administratively responsible for all of the Marines attached to the unit.

Our local community started experiencing a cluster of childhood leukemia cases. The rate rapidly grew to forty times the national average, and scientific experts were unable to identify a cause. Given the uncertainty and risk to our Navy and Marine families, I suggested that we develop plans to enable families with children to relocate to adjacent communities until experts could identify a probable cause.

My suggestion was met with disdain by the admiral. They were "looking into it," and "that's all I needed to know." When I pushed, I was basically told to be quiet or else they would initiate actions that would adversely affect my career. I sensed an attempt to sweep things under the rug, and headwinds were blowing. But my gut was telling me we needed to do something to take care of our families while the experts searched for answers. As the days turned into weeks and the number of cases grew with no explanations and little information, parents' emotions turned from uncertainty to worry to anger. I was facing a moral and emotional dilemma.

One Friday morning, as my dad's words echoed in my mind and the guy in the glass stared back at me, I decided to leverage my position as the senior Marine and engage my administrative chain of command. I knew my Navy operational chain of command had told me to cease and desist, but my conscience told me otherwise.

I called the chief medical officer at Headquarters, U.S. Marine Corps, seeking information and advice regarding childhood leukemia clusters. His first question was, "Why haven't I heard about this before now?" When I explained that I wasn't sure why, he promised to do some research and get back to me. I sensed from the tone of his voice that he was uncomfortable with the information I had just shared with him.

Four hours later, my headwinds turned into a hurricane. Apparently, the admiral, who was on vacation, got a call from the Chief of Naval Operations instructing him to return to his office and explain what was going on. I found out later that the chief medical officer immediately informed the Commandant of the Marine Corps, which prompted a conversation with the Chief of Naval Operations. Furthermore, the Commandant decided to pay for Marine families with children to move out of the local area if they wished. It would be hard at this point for the admiral not to follow suit with our Navy families.

Upon the admiral's return, I was directed to report to his office immediately, where I was berated for over an hour and told that I would never recover from this. Then he made sure of it on my next performance evaluation. In full transparency, I have to admit there were times when I wondered whether doing the right thing was really the right thing to do.

But in the background, there were people going to bat for me. I still get emotional thinking about it, because this was such a defining moment in my military career that could have gone either way. My immediate boss, our unit's commanding officer, took a lot of heat for defending my actions. A few Marine generals got involved behind the scenes. And the Assistant Commandant of the Marine Corps wrote a special performance evaluation on my behalf, refuting the admiral's adverse appraisal. Thanks to all of them I recovered, and I learned a lot about courage in the process.

I also learned a lot about the extremes of good and bad leadership through that experience. I'm often asked, "Can you learn anything from bad leaders?" My answer is unequivocally, "Yes." In fact, I recommend that leaders keep a "leadership lessons learned" notebook with two sections—"things to do as a leader" in the front, and "things to never do" in the back. Unfortunately, a few of my notebooks are much fuller in the back than the front. Perhaps you could say the same about some of your experiences. But many of the best leadership lessons I've ever learned have come from the "things I'll never do as a leader" section. I think there's a silver lining in every negative leadership experience if it helps you become a better leader.

The cause of the childhood leukemia cluster has never been determined. I have my theories, but I won't elaborate here. What I will share is that the admiral was promoted and placed in charge of an education and training organization with a large staff that included both Navy and Marine personnel.

I soon learned through the grapevine that morale among the staff there was declining due to the admiral's abrasive style, and that he was particularly adversarial toward Marines. I also heard that he had displayed this type of behavior in the past, even before my encounter with him. At least I wasn't the only one, I guess.

One evening after a local night on the town, the admiral was walking back to the base with a group of friends, all of them in civilian clothes. As they approached the gate just beyond a sign that read, "100% ID Check in Progress," the Marine corporal on duty asked them to show identification. Disgusted that the corporal didn't recognize him, the admiral grabbed the guard and shoved his identification card in his face. Reacting instinctively on his Marine guard training, the corporal pepper-sprayed the admiral, sending him into a fetal position on the pavement.

The next day, out of retribution, the admiral transferred the corporal to an undesirable assignment. This eventually sparked a formal investigation by the Inspector General, which uncovered a pattern of toxic leadership. The admiral was ultimately forced to resign and retire.

On multiple levels, that's a painful story for me to tell. First, I don't like to highlight others' leadership shortcomings. I know how hard leadership is and I have enough failures of my own, so I don't want to judge. That's why I intentionally left out names and specific locations in order to be as vague as practical while still illustrating the lessons learned.

Second, it tested me emotionally. My heart went out to the families of children in the local community and to our military families that were stationed there, who were coping with uncertainty and fear on a daily basis. Concern for the safety of my own children and our family's emotional well-being weighed on me heavily. And my heart still grieves for the families and children who had to battle leukemia, especially the ones who lost the fight.

Third, it tested me professionally. There were days when I was sure I would never fly or lead in the military again. There were days when I doubted my conscience. And even worse, there were days when I questioned whether doing the right thing was worth it.

But I believe everything happens for a reason. That experience helped develop my character. It helped build my confidence in what good leadership looks like. And it helped strengthen my courage to do the right thing, regardless of the consequences. These three lessons prepared me for future leadership challenges in ways that I couldn't have imagined at the time. I hope they'll encourage you to take the high road the next time you're tested. It will be the one less traveled, but it will make all the difference.

Competence Builds a Culture of Trust

I believe the second vital leadership quality for creating a high-performing culture of trust is *competence*. I've always translated competence as *doing things right*. In my experience, competence is crucial to creating a high-performing culture because people tend to trust and follow other people who "know their stuff," work hard to improve, and lead by example.

Doing Things Right

As a young Marine pilot, I admired squadron commanding officers who led from the front. They set the example through their ethical and professional conduct, never considering themselves above the rules. They were also technically and tactically proficient, always willing and able to lead the toughest missions. They were committed to self-improvement and were humble enough to admit their mistakes while holding themselves to a higher standard than those they led. Simply put, they walked their talk and their actions spoke louder than their words. If actions actually could speak, everyone would hear, "Follow me and do what I do, because I want to show you how to succeed."

> Competence is crucial to creating a high-performing culture because people tend to trust and follow other people who "know their stuff," work hard to improve, and lead by example.

As a result, every pilot in the squadron wanted to fly with them. If "the balloon went up" and we were called into combat, everyone wanted the commanding officer (CO) to lead the first mission and hoped they could fly on the skipper's wing into harm's way. Moreover, pilots in other squadrons who weren't so fortunate to have a CO who led from the front wanted to be in the squadron of a skipper who did. It didn't take long for me to realize that leading from the front is really important, and I hoped I could become that type of leader.

But as I progressed through my career and my scope of responsibility grew, I quickly discovered how difficult it is to maintain technical and tactical proficiency as you move up the ranks. Not only do your daily challenges grow in number, they also grow in complexity. If you're not careful, "urgent" things can rapidly overtake the important things. However, leading by example was important. I couldn't ignore the question, "How can I ask others to pursue operational excellence and manage risk if I am not willing to do the same myself?"

The answer was that I couldn't. So I had to intentionally prioritize my time in order to invest in training and growth opportunities that would help me maintain technical and tactical proficiency in a rapidly changing environment. I often wondered whether the investment was worth the effort, especially since my plate was full with other competing priorities. Additionally, I wasn't able to maintain the same level of proficiency that I once could achieve when I was more junior and had more time to devote to training, so I sometimes wondered, "Does it really make a difference?"

I learned the answer to that question during my final assignment in the Marine Corps. As the commanding officer of a Marine aircraft group (MAG) in Beaufort, South Carolina, I was the colonel in charge of six FA-18 squadrons and was affectionately referred to as "the old man" by all of the junior pilots in the MAG. I couldn't disagree, because years earlier I was a junior pilot in the same MAG, and I remember standing in formation listening to the MAG CO talk to us while thinking to myself, *That guy is old.* Now I was "that guy."

In an effort to maintain technical and tactical competence, I made it a priority to fly and train with all six squadrons on a rotating basis. In the process, I did my best to lead by example tactically and debrief lessons that I had learned throughout my career that I hoped could help them succeed in their careers. I know I wasn't always successful. But over time, I found myself being scheduled to fly more and more with junior pilots whose collateral duty was writing the daily flight schedule.

Generally speaking, squadron schedule writers have the "power of the pen" when it comes to determining who flies with whom. They could have easily scheduled themselves to fly with someone else, but I was exceedingly humbled and honored when they wanted to fly with "the old man." These occasions afforded me unique opportunities to mentor our next generation of leaders and provided me with rare insights about the pulse of our organization on the front lines, which helped me to be a more informed and influential leader.

Pursue professional competence and lead by example.

Competence Enables Your Team to Trust Your Actions

Through that experience, combined with feedback and many other observations over the years, I learned that working hard to pursue professional competence and lead by example results in a huge return on investment in the form of professional credibility, which enables your team to *trust your actions*. And trust is the center of gravity of a high-performing culture. Therefore, it's important to continuously ask yourself, "How well do I 'know my stuff' regarding my team's core mission, and how hard am I working to improve?" Because the teams that I've seen rise to the occasion and perform under pressure had a leader who was committed to professional competence, which raised the bar throughout the entire organization.

Composure Builds a Culture of Trust

I believe the third vital leadership quality for creating a culture of trust is *composure*. I've always translated composure as *setting the right tone*. By the right tone I mean an enthusiastic, positive tone that sees problems not as annoyances, but rather as opportunities to lead. I've found it helpful to frequently remind myself and my team that bad things will inevitably happen. But how we respond in those situations is critically important for two reasons: first, because true character is revealed under adversity; and second, because how we as leaders respond to adversity will significantly affect how our team responds.

Setting the Right Tone

I'm sure you can think of a leader who doesn't respond very well

> Trust is the center of gravity of a high-performing culture.

to bad news, adversity, or pressure. It only takes a few times for someone like this to "shoot the messenger" before everyone stops bringing them any bad news. And then it doesn't take long until the leader becomes disconnected from what is really going on within the organization. Moreover, a leader's negative response to adversity tends to be contagious. And even worse, when a leader panics under pressure it can spread like wildfire throughout the entire team.

I experienced this firsthand just a few weeks after my "ride along" medevac mission in Iraq. As a battle captain in our aircraft wing's tactical air command center, in addition to coordinating medical evacuations, I was also responsible for orchestrating operations for a team of 5,000 aviation and logistics professionals with 200 aircraft providing air support for the 30,000 Marines and Soldiers deployed throughout western Iraq.

One afternoon, I was notified that there was a large mob forming outside the front gate of our base. When I glanced at the large video screen in the command center that provided live feed from a drone overhead, I could see in the distance two white sedans converging toward the mob at high rates of speed from different directions along dusty roads.

A few minutes later, we started receiving reports of incoming mortar fire in the north sector of our airfield, where most of our helicopters were parked. And just when I thought things couldn't get worse, six simultaneous firefights erupted throughout our area of responsibility. Casualties began to mount, and we rapidly started running short of medevac aircraft. I realized we were experiencing a coordinated attack. To be honest, I began to sense the urge to panic.

Then I had a flashback to three years earlier when I was in a classroom listening to a combat leadership lecture by retired U.S. Army Lieutenant General Harold "Hal" Moore, who wrote a book in 1992 titled *We Were Soldiers Once . . . and Young*. It was about his experiences as then Lieutenant Colonel Moore when he was the commanding officer of the First Battalion, Seventh

Cavalry Regiment in the Battle of the Ia Drang Valley in Vietnam in 1965. In 2002 the book was made into a movie by the same name, with Mel Gibson playing Lieutenant Colonel Hal Moore.

What I remember most about Lieutenant General Moore's comments that day is when he told us that if we ever found ourselves in a combat leadership situation, there would inevitably come a time when lives would be on the line and the pressure would be so great that we would feel a natural urge to panic. And when that moment occurred, he encouraged us to take a deep breath, speak calmly and clearly, and do our best to make the most of a bad situation . . . because otherwise it would only get worse.

I realized I was in that moment Lieutenant General Moore had talked about three years earlier. So I huddled up my team of air support directors in the command center and quickly asked them to do two things.

First, I acknowledged that we were running out of resources to adequately respond to all of the requests for close air support and medical evacuations that were rushing in. Because time was of the essence, I asked them to think outside the box to find ways to maximize our limited resources in order to save as many people as possible, and keep me updated so I could have their backs. Second, I reminded them to take a deep breath and remain calm on the radio when directing air support, because if anyone sensed that we were panicking in the command center, it could spread like wildfire throughout the battlespace.

As I was launching our quick-reaction force toward the front gate, our fixed-wing (jet and propeller aircraft) air support director reported that there was an FA-18 on final approach with a little extra fuel, and he had asked the aircrew to conduct a high-speed, low-altitude "show of force" over the mob at the front gate. As I looked up at the screen displaying the live video feed from the drone overhead, I watched the crowd crouch and then begin to scatter as the jet passed just over their heads at nearly the speed of sound.

Evidently caught off guard by what was happening, both white sedans stopped about a mile from the gate and eventually turned around. A few minutes later, the quick-reaction force found a third white sedan parked near the gate. Upon further inspection, they discovered the trunk was filled with explosives, and they were able to quickly neutralize it before anyone was injured or killed. We later learned that the third sedan was part of a coordinated suicide attack, along with the other two sedans previously speeding toward the mob.

In the meantime, our attack helicopter director informed me that he had diverted a flight of two AH-1 Cobras toward the area from where we suspected the incoming mortar fire was originating. Apparently not wishing to attract any attention from the Cobras, the mortar fire ceased, which bought us some precious time to launch more helicopters to assist with air support and medical evacuations.

Finally, our transport helicopter director briefed me that she had asked four CH-53 Super Stallions on a logistical support mission to conduct a hasty landing and disembark their cargo. They set up a temporary security perimeter and then switched missions to provide vital medevac support.

I wish I could tell you we saved everyone that evening. Unfortunately, I can't. But I can tell you that our team made the most of a bad situation in the midst of a life-and-death crisis. I am extremely grateful for Lieutenant General Moore's words of wisdom three years earlier. His lesson is one that I've tried to emulate and pass on to other leaders ever since.

Composure Enables Your Team to Trust Your Emotions

The tone you set when faced with difficult challenges will definitely influence how your team responds to adversity. Bad things will inevitably happen, and bad news rarely gets better with time. Be approachable, and encourage the members of your team to bring bad news to you so you can problem-solve together. I can remember a number of conversations that started with, "Sir, you just can't make this stuff up."

When that happens, take a deep breath and maintain your composure. Use the adversity as an opportunity to help develop your team's character. Focus on what happened, what they are doing about it, and how they can prevent it from happening in the future. Maintaining your composure as a leader will enable your team to *trust your emotions*. As a result, I think you'll be pleasantly surprised by how much more tuned in you are to the pulse of your organization, by the increased level of trust it creates within your team, and by the positive effect it has on your culture.

> The tone you set when faced with difficult challenges will definitely influence how your team responds to adversity.

Summary

In this chapter we introduced the first essential focus area in the *leadership triad*: *culture*. Culture is essential for leading a high-performing team because it forms the lens through which your team members view each other and your team's mission. Your culture is the set of shared attitudes, values, goals, and practices that characterizes your team. It's where your team's mind-sets and behaviors intersect. In other words, your culture defines the essence of who your team is.

A high-performing culture can be summarized in one word: *trust*. The key question at the beginning of the chapter was, "How can you create a high-performing culture of trust within your team?" We answered this question by unpacking three key leadership qualities described as "the three C's" of a high-performing cul-ture: *character*, *competence*, and *composure*. These three leadership qualities will define the quality of your culture. In other words, the quality of your culture starts with you.

> To build a high-performing culture, focus on the content of your character, the caliber of your competence, and the capacity of your composure.

To build a high-performing culture, focus on the content of your *character*, the caliber of your *competence*, and the capacity of your *composure*. In your day-to-day leadership responsibilities, this means being dedicated to *doing the right thing, doing things right,* and *setting the right tone*. When you as a leader demonstrate strong character, I as a member of your team can trust your *intentions*, knowing that you are committed to always trying to *do the right thing*. When you are competent, I can trust your *actions*, knowing that I can depend on you to always try to *do things right*. And when you are composed, I can trust your *emotions*, knowing that I can count on you to always try to *set a calm and positive tone*.

When you as a leader do these three things right, you inspire your people to do the same. This creates a culture where the members of your team can trust each other at all costs. And when this happens, they will do almost anything to keep from letting each other down.

QUESTIONS FOR REFLECTION

- How would you describe your team's culture?
- What key areas do you need to focus on to improve it?
- What leadership qualities do you need to improve to develop a stronger culture of trust?

CHAPTER 2

PEOPLE

"To handle yourself, use your head; to handle others, use your heart."

—ELEANOR ROOSEVELT

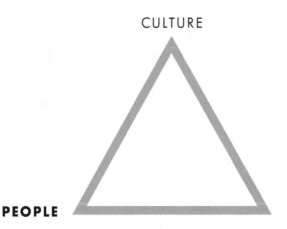

Bill Crawford was a dormitory janitor at the U.S. Air Force Academy in the 1970s. While cadets immersed themselves in the constant demands of academics, athletics, and military duties, Bill quietly mopped floors, cleaned toilets, and emptied trash cans. Bill took pride in his job, and the dorm was always spotless. Perhaps that's one of the reasons most of the cadets barely noticed him.

Bill was not physically impressive. Maybe that's another reason few cadets noticed him. He moved a little more slowly than they did, and he even shuffled a bit. His gray hair made him look old and maybe even a bit out of touch.

James Moschgat was one of those cadets who barely noticed Bill during his first three years at the Air Force Academy. Then one Saturday afternoon during his senior year while studying World War II history, a particular story grabbed his attention.

Private William Crawford, a U.S. Army soldier from Pueblo, Colorado, and a member of the 36th Infantry Division, was awarded the Medal of Honor "for conspicuous gallantry and intrepidity at risk of life above and beyond the call of duty in action with the enemy near Altavilla, Italy, 13 September 1943."[4] On his own initiative, Crawford single-handedly attacked multiple enemy positions in the face of intense machine gun fire, which enabled his company's advance. "You're not going to believe this," James exclaimed to his roommate, "but I think our janitor is a Medal of Honor recipient."

Early Monday morning James found Bill and showed him the story, asking if that was him. "Yep, that's me," Bill quietly responded. James then asked, "Why didn't you tell us?" Bill simply said, "That was one day in my life, and it happened a long time ago."

Word got out quickly, and the cadets in James's squadron began to see Bill in a completely different light. He was a humble hero in their midst, and his presence garnered a whole new level of respect. The same cadets who once passed Bill in the hallway with barely a glance, now greeted him with a heartfelt, "Good morning, Mr. Crawford." They found themselves stopping to talk with Bill more frequently and began inviting him to attend their formal functions as a special guest.

Many years later in his Air Force career, Colonel James Moschgat shared this story along with the leadership lessons he learned from it. Among them are: be cautious of labels, everyone deserves respect, courtesy makes a difference, take time to know your people, and leaders should be humble.[5] In other words, never take people for granted.

I am sometimes asked, "What's the difference between management and leadership?" My simple answer is that management is process-centric, and leadership is people-centric. That's why the second essential focus area that I

> Management is process-centric, and leadership is people-centric.

believe is critical for leading a consistently high-performing team is every organization's most important and valuable asset—your *people*. And in my experience, focusing on your people starts with *respect*.

Respect Your People

In over three decades of leadership, I have never met anyone who looked up to someone who looked down on them. This is the reason why one of my non-negotiables on every team that I've had the privilege of leading is that we treat everyone with fairness, dignity, and respect—with no exceptions.

I learned the value of respect from my mom, Joyce Robinson. She taught me the importance of treating others how you want to be treated. I remember her frequently admonishing my brothers and me when we were growing up: "Be kind to everyone you meet, especially the janitors and secretaries." She didn't know about Bill Crawford at the time, but her point was that in every "insignificant" position is an important person.

At its core, I believe respecting your people boils down to having genuine compassion and concern for their welfare. I've also found that genuine compassion and concern for others are often honed in the crucible of our own adversity and failure.

Earning Your Team's Respect Starts with Respecting Your People

I'll never forget my first aerial dogfighting training mission. I was a new FA-18 pilot, just beginning to learn how to tactically employ the aircraft. As fate would have it, I was scheduled to fight one of the best adversary pilots in the United States Navy and Marine Corps. He had decades of experience flying the F-5 Tiger—a sleek, supersonic fighter with a camouflage paint scheme that was used to resemble enemy aircraft for training purposes. Although the F-5 was not as nimble and powerful as my FA-18, it was nonetheless formidable and even intimidating, especially when flown by an experienced pilot against a rookie like me.

> I have never met anyone who looked up to someone who looked down on them.

To assist with my training, I had an instructor pilot in my back seat to help teach me how to maneuver in three dimensions under seven and a half times the force of gravity and make decisions at the speed of sound. As you might expect, it didn't take very long before the F-5 was camped out at my six o'clock. No matter what I did, I found myself continuously looking over my shoulder while I remained in the F-5's gun sight.

After nearly a minute of this, my instructor in the back seat began to get a little animated. After a few more minutes, his animation turned into screaming. I was in the F-5's gun sight for almost an hour that day. And it's the only time in my life when I've heard someone scream for an entire hour. At one point I was tempted to pull the ejection handle to get him out of the jet. Fortunately, better judgment prevailed.

You would think the screaming would stop when we landed and shut the engines down. But it didn't. Even as we walked back into the ready room, he continued berating and belittling me in front of my peers and other instructors who were waiting for their flights.

I smile whenever I tell this story, because it's easy to laugh about it now. But it wasn't very funny at the time. In fact, it was one of the most humiliating flights in my entire career. However, looking back I wouldn't trade it for the world. Because although I didn't learn anything that day about dogfighting, I learned a lot about the value of respect. I learned a lot about the significance of praising people in public, but reprimanding them in private. And I learned a lot about the importance of looking beyond someone's performance and focusing on their potential. This was one of those "crucible moments" that paid huge dividends for me later as an instructor and a leader, because it taught me that earning our people's respect starts with *respecting our people*.

> I learned a lot about the importance of looking beyond someone's performance and focusing on their potential.

Know Your People

The second level of focusing on your people is *knowing* them. I don't mean just knowing their names, I mean *really knowing* them.

I think one of the most significant effects of the information technology revolution that has evolved over the past two decades is that while it's far easier to communicate more broadly with people today through e-mail, social media, and other forms of virtual communication, it is more challenging to communicate with meaningful depth. It's difficult to read emotions through the screen of a computer or cell phone.

But the quality of our communication is not the only challenge. American adults today spend on average more than ten hours per day connected to some form of media.[6] Knowing your people requires quantity as well as quality time. That means competing with the constant flow of information that individuals are nearly continuously connected to. For these reasons, I'll go out on a limb here and assert that you can't adequately know your people and lead them effectively from behind a desk.

> You can't adequately know your people and lead them effectively from behind a desk.

Your Team Will Know How Much You Care

This lesson about the importance of really knowing your people was tragically reinforced for me when I was transitioning to my final assignment in the Marine Corps. I was working for the Chairman of the Joint Chiefs of Staff in Washington, DC, when I learned that I had been selected to command the Marine aircraft group in South Carolina that I mentioned earlier, where I would be leading 2,500 people supporting operations around the globe. Needless to say, I was extremely honored and excited about the opportunity.

Two Mondays before officially taking command of the aircraft group, my excitement turned to devastation when I learned there were two suicides in the unit over the weekend. It ripped my heart out. Even worse, it was an increasing trend throughout the Marine Corps, where we were beginning to experience more deaths due to suicide than from combat operations in Iraq and Afghanistan combined.

I soon began working closely with mental health professionals and chaplains, as well as friends and family members of the deceased, to try to understand why anyone with so much potential would take their own life. In my search for answers, something became very clear to me.

In the midst of mass communication and information saturation, we had gotten away from the basics of really knowing our people. As a result, many of our people felt disconnected from a support network they could depend on when they encountered professional, financial, or relational challenges.

So we got back to basics. I re-energized a program that I had started five years earlier as an FA-18 training squadron commander in San Diego, after experiencing a wave of disciplinary challenges and driving under the influence offenses. It was based on the principles of small unit leadership and was designed around four-person "fire teams" that are common within infantry squads.

Every member of the aircraft group was assigned to a team comprised of three individuals with similar experience and rank. Each team was assigned a "team leader" who was accountable for their welfare. Three team leaders with similar experience and rank then formed a team that had a slightly more senior team leader, and so on. Ultimately all 2,500 individuals in the aircraft group were assigned to a team with a team leader who was responsible for *knowing* them and looking out for their physical, mental, moral, and emotional welfare.

We held team leaders accountable for *really knowing* their people; not just their name, but everything about them. We expected team leaders to know about their team members' family, where they grew up, their hobbies, professional aspirations, personal ambitions, what motivated them, what discouraged them, their hopes, their fears, their challenges, and how we could help them overcome those challenges to achieve their personal and professional goals.

Before a team member departed work for weekend liberty or personal leave, team leaders were expected to mentor them about potential risks and mitigations, as well as remind them that help was just a phone call away if they needed anything. We were serious about empowering team leaders to lead, while simultaneously holding them accountable if any of their team members got into trouble.

We also reached out to family members who knew their Marines best, in order to help us know them better. We thanked them for entrusting their family member to our Marine Corps family, and asked for their trust in assisting us to help their Marine. We asked them to let us know if there was anything we could do to better support a family member who might be facing difficult challenges, or struggling with depression or suicidal thoughts. And we promised that anything they shared would not in any way negatively affect their Marine's career.

Simultaneously, we worked hard to ensure a culture of caring within the aircraft group. One of the most sacred elements of the U.S. warrior ethos is that we never leave anyone behind on the battlefield. We acknowledged that psychological wounds can be just as, if not more, damaging and painful as physical wounds, and we vowed to leave no one behind on the battlefield of life.

We received a lot of calls and e-mails from family members. In each case, we were able to work through the Marine's team leader to provide additional support. Frequently the support was just assuring them that they could talk to their team leader about their problems, and that the organization had their back. Sometimes it was connecting them to professionals with more specialized skills and counseling experience. Many times our chaplains were exceptionally helpful. I can't quantify the difference it made, but I can tell you it was huge.

> Knowing your people is the key to understanding their challenges and helping them through.

I feel exceptionally blessed to be able to tell you that not only did we experience a drastic decline in the number of suicides in the aircraft group, but I also saw the organization reach a new level of morale and performance.

I tell this story because it's one of the clearest examples I've ever experienced regarding the importance of knowing your people. One of our greatest organizational challenges was young people being so discouraged by their own personal challenges that they were willing to take their own lives. Perhaps your people challenges are less extreme. But I can guarantee you every one of your people has challenges. *Knowing* your people is the key to understanding these challenges and helping them through.

In hindsight, I honestly believe that one of the main reasons we were able to work through many of our challenges and see a rise in morale and performance throughout the organization is because everyone knew that someone cared. Which brings us to the third level of focusing on your people.

Take Care of Your People

In my experience, *taking care* of your people boils down to a personal commitment to looking out for their welfare. It's about making sure they can trust that you have their back. And it's about being an available mentor who is approachable enough that they feel comfortable coming to you with their problems because they know you have their best interests at heart.

> Taking care of your people boils down to a personal commitment to looking out for their welfare.

At the highest level, it starts by inspiring them with a sense of meaning and purpose as a result of helping them understand how they fit into the big picture and are contributing to the team's overall goals. At the most practical level, it involves finding out what makes their life hard, and then doing something about it.

Your Team Will Take Care of You

Not long after I returned from my rookie combat deployment to the Persian Gulf aboard the USS *Abraham Lincoln*, I was honored and excited to learn that I had been selected to attend the United States Navy Fighter Weapons School (TOPGUN) in Miramar, California. If you've seen the original *Top Gun* movie that was filmed in Miramar and released in 1986, I hate to disappoint you . . . but in typical Hollywood fashion, the movie is not exactly like the real thing. We didn't ride motorcycles down the runway and play beach volleyball. On the contrary, it was one of the most professional, high-performing organizations I've ever been associated with.

But lest I digress, suffice it to say that when I returned to my new squadron following my graduation from TOPGUN, I was assigned to the position of pilot training officer. In this role I was responsible for training all of the rookie pilots who had just checked into the squadron. It was one of the best jobs that I ever had in my career, because it was so rewarding to invest in others and watch them grow in their capabilities and confidence.

One of those rookie pilots was a junior captain named Patrick Guinee. He had an intangible maturity about him that was obvious to most. Our commanding officer recognized that immediately, and he put Patrick in charge of the largest division in our squadron's aircraft maintenance department.

As the airframes division officer, Patrick was responsible for fifty of the toughest and roughest Marines in the unit. They were a diverse group of men and women from all over America who loved to bend metal and fix jets more than almost anything else. Many of them came from challenging backgrounds and lacked positive role models. But all of them would have followed Patrick anywhere and done anything for him.

One day when we finished our debrief following a training flight, I sat across the table from Patrick and asked him a question. "Your Marines would follow you anywhere and do absolutely anything for you," I observed. "What is your secret?"

I'll never forget his answer. Patrick looked me straight in the eyes and said, "There is no secret. In fact, it's really simple. Bottom line, your people have to know beyond a doubt that you care more about their welfare than you care about your own."

Your people have to know beyond a doubt that you care more about their welfare than you care about your own.

I'm ashamed to tell you that I immediately sunk in my chair, because at that point in my career I couldn't say that about myself. But I was determined to change, because I aspired to have what Patrick was able to inspire in his people. So I began to intentionally focus on improving as a leader. And in the course of that journey, I discovered two very important things.

First, if we want to grow as a leader, we need to humbly acknowledge our gaps and seek out mentors who can help us improve. If you don't have a small network of mentors that can help you grow, start developing one now. And second, if you take care of your people, they will take care of you by doing whatever it takes to accomplish the mission.

> If you take care of your people, they will take care of you by doing whatever it takes to accomplish the mission.

Convincing your people that you care more about their welfare than your own requires sacrifice. But it is worth it. In fact, it's some of the best advice I've ever received and one of the most valuable leadership lessons I've ever learned. Thankfully, Patrick helped me learn this lesson early in my career, and he has remained a faithful friend and mentor ever since.

Summary

Focusing on your people is one of the hardest things you'll ever do as a leader. As James Moschgat learned through his relationship with Bill Crawford at the U.S. Air Force Academy, it requires humility so that you don't take anyone for granted, especially the heroes in our midst who impeccably but quietly do their jobs. It requires selflessness and self-sacrifice. It means putting others' interests ahead of your own. That's not easy.

However, if you can focus on *respecting* your people by treating them how you would want to be treated and by having genuine compassion and concern for their welfare, you will in turn earn their respect. If you focus on *knowing* your people by learning about their challenges and helping them through, they will know how much you care. And if you focus on *taking care* of your people by leaving no doubt that you care more about their welfare than your own, they will take care of you by doing whatever it takes to accomplish the mission. Which brings us to essential focus area number three.

QUESTIONS FOR REFLECTION

- Would everyone on your team say they feel respected?
- What can you start doing to know your people better?
- What can you start doing to take care of your people better?

CHAPTER 3

MISSION

"The main thing is to keep the
main thing the main thing."

—T. F. TENNEY

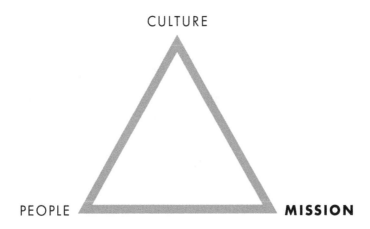

CULTURE

PEOPLE

MISSION

Fred Haise was a Marine fighter pilot and test pilot
from Biloxi, Mississippi, with a degree in aeronautical engineering from the University of Oklahoma. Jack Swigert was an Air
Force fighter pilot and test pilot from Denver who played football
for the University of Colorado and graduated with a degree in
mechanical engineering. Jim Lovell was a Navy fighter pilot and
test pilot with a bachelor of science degree from the U.S. Naval
Academy. Together they formed the crew of Apollo 13.[7]

The mission of Apollo 13 was to demonstrate a precision
manned lunar landing and conduct lunar exploration. It was the

seventh manned mission in the Apollo space program, and the third planned to land on the moon.[8]

On April 11, 1970, after more than 1,000 hours of mission training, including over 400 hours of simulation, the crew launched toward space from Cape Canaveral aboard a Saturn V rocket with Jim Lovell as the mission commander. Fifty-six hours later, as Apollo 13 reached an altitude of 200,000 miles above Earth, the crew heard a sharp bang and felt a strong vibration. An associated warning light prompted Jim Lovell to utter the famous words, "Houston, we've had a problem."[9]

They soon discovered that one of the two oxygen tanks in the spacecraft's service module had exploded, causing the other tank to fail as well. Since the module's fuel cells needed oxygen to operate, they were also losing power. Apollo 13's mission had just changed from exploration to survival.[10]

Gene Kranz, an aerospace engineer and former Air Force fighter pilot, was NASA's lead flight director for the mission control team in Houston. Working closely with the flight crew, Gene and his team assessed that there wasn't enough power remaining to turn the spacecraft around and get it pointed directly back toward Earth. So they developed a plan to continue toward the moon and "loop around" it, using the gravitational force to "slingshot" the crew back to Earth.[11]

Gene directed the crew to use the oxygen and battery power from the spacecraft's lunar module. But given the long route around the moon, he knew the crew would have to conserve every bit of both to make it home alive. After four days of intense problem-solving and constant teamwork between mission control and the flight crew, Apollo 13 safely splashed down in the South Pacific.[12]

Jerry Bostick, who grew up in Fred Haise's home state of Mississippi, was a NASA engineer during the Apollo 13 mission. Several years later he was asked in an interview what it was like inside mission control, and whether there were times when anyone panicked. His answer was, "No, when bad things happened, we just calmly laid out all the options, and failure was not one of them"—which inspired the iconic line, "Failure is not an option" in the 1995 film, *Apollo 13*.[13]

Although it's unlikely your team is in the business of moon landings, it's highly likely that your mission is critical and failure is not an option for you. That's why the third essential focus area for leading a consistently high-performing team is your *mission*. And when I discuss what it takes to have a high-performing mission focus, I like to emphasize "the three P's."

Prioritization Sets the Foundation for Mission Success

The first "P" is *prioritization*. In addition to the challenges brought about by the information technology revolution I mentioned earlier related to knowing and communicating with your people with meaningful depth, I think there is a second important effect that makes leadership especially challenging in the information age. Specifically, I'm referring to the volume and speed at which information flows onto your plate.

Between e-mail, phone, text, instant messaging, video conferencing, social media, the internet, and an ever-expanding list of other applications, information saturation has become the norm. Most of the

When everything is a priority, nothing is a priority.

time your plate is overflowing, and it can feel like everything is a priority. But as the old saying goes, "When everything is a priority, nothing is a priority."[14]

Help Your Team Keep the Main Thing the Main Thing

This lesson was especially reinforced for me in 2009 when I was transitioning from the Pentagon to my final assignment as the Marine aircraft group commander in South Carolina. It's customary for commanding officers in the military to develop and distribute a "philosophy of command." This is typically a one-page leadership philosophy or "leader's intent" for the organization, so that everyone knows the commander's vision and expectations for the unit (we'll discuss this topic in more depth in the next chapter).

> The unit was focused on being good at so many priorities, that it was at risk of being average at best at what mattered most.

As I began my due diligence and mission analysis to draft my leader's intent, a familiar pattern began to emerge. Like many organizations, it seemed like the unit was focused on being good at so many priorities that it was at risk of being average at best at what mattered most.

To drill deeper, I researched all of the requirements that the unit was accountable for in the form of directives and orders from higher headquarters. The list added up to approximately fifty mandatory requirements throughout the year, with various time commitments for each. When I added up the total time requirement and divided it by the total number of people in the aircraft group, the result was an average of twenty-three hours per person per day. That didn't include eating or sleeping. Clearly something had to give.

So I began whittling down all fifty requirements into five core priorities that I believed were critical for us to excel at what mattered most. I've found that it's important for an organization's priorities to flow from its purpose. Our purpose was our mission, and our mission was to be prepared to win in combat. Around this purpose revolved our five core priorities: aircrew training, aircraft readiness, maintenance training, risk management, and family readiness.

My philosophy was that winning in combat required well trained, tactically proficient aircrew. Aircrew training depended upon our ability to generate training flights with ready aircraft, which in turn required quality maintenance. Sustained success in these areas required an underlying foundation of sound judgment and prudent risk management in order to maximize combat preparedness while simultaneously protecting our people and preserving our resources. And finally, all of these priorities directly depended on the morale and welfare of our most valuable assets—each and every Marine, Sailor, government civilian, and family member in the aircraft group.

> It's important for an organization's priorities to flow from its purpose.

In order to remain focused on these five core areas, however, I had to accept risk in the remaining forty-five "priorities." But I am so glad I did, because six months later all nine squadrons in the aircraft group were called upon to deploy nearly simultaneously to the four corners of the globe: from Iraq to Afghanistan to Japan and to aircraft carriers everywhere between.

Looking back, I am convinced that had I not prioritized, some of those units would not have not been successful in their mission. And a few of them would not have brought everyone home safely. But due to extraordinary leadership and focus by the commanding officers of those squadrons, they performed remarkably in their missions and brought everyone home safely.

Perhaps what is most surprising to me is that my boss never asked me about the other forty-five priorities. This reinforced for me how important it is in today's world of information saturation to diligently protect and shield our teams by helping them prioritize, so that they can stay focused on what's most important and "keep the main thing the main thing."

Preparation Gives Form to Mission Success

I loved basketball growing up. I played in high school, and for two years at the U.S. Naval Academy as a member of the junior varsity team (to avoid any confusion with "The Admiral" who went on to become an NBA All Star, I was known as "little Dave" or "the other David Robinson" in the Class of 1987 at Annapolis).

Because of my connection to basketball, I always admired the late, great coach John Wooden. He coached the UCLA Bruins to ten NCAA basketball championships in a twelve-year span in the 1960s and 70s, including seven consecutive national championships and eighty-eight straight victories at one point. As a result, in 1999 ESPN presented him their Coach of the Century award. And each year the John R. Wooden Award is presented to the most outstanding player in men's and women's college basketball, which "The Admiral" received in 1987.

I've always had tremendous respect for John Wooden as a coach. But I have even more respect for him as a person and a leader. John Wooden was the consummate teacher and mentor who instilled values and character into his players, which he credited as a key reason for his consistently high-performing teams over such an extended period of time.[15]

Immediately following my junior year as a midshipman at Annapolis, I was assigned to San Diego for summer training. While I was there, I learned that Coach Wooden was conducting a basketball clinic one Saturday at Pepperdine University in Malibu, just west of Los Angeles. On a whim, I rented a car and drove up the Pacific Coast Highway to the Pepperdine campus, atop the beautiful palisades overlooking the Pacific Ocean.

With no plan other than sheer curiosity, I found an unlocked side door, quietly entered the gymnasium, and took a seat in the closest set of bleachers near the door. On the court in front of me, the "Wizard of Westwood" was running a few dozen men in their mid-thirties through a series of ball-handling drills. Undoubtedly they were huge John Wooden fans like myself and had likely paid handsomely for the opportunity to be coached by him for a day.

A few minutes later, one of Coach Wooden's assistants approached me from across the court. He asked who I was and what I was doing there. When I told him my name was David Robinson and that I was in California from the U.S. Naval Academy for summer training, he smiled as if to say, "Yeah right."

As he walked back across the court, I began wondering how much trouble I had just created for myself. He whispered something into Coach Wooden's ear, and then Coach Wooden whispered something in return. The assistant walked back over to me and said, "Coach Wooden wants to see you in his office when the clinic is over." Uh-oh.

When the clinic ended, the assistant came over and escorted me to an office adjacent to the gymnasium. As I nervously entered, John Wooden humbly introduced himself, gently put me at ease, and then asked me to sit down. I wasn't sure what to expect, but I certainly didn't expect what happened next.

Coach Wooden spent the next hour mentoring and pouring life lessons into a young college junior that he had only just met because I sneaked into his gym. He shared stories with me about his time as a lieutenant in the U.S. Navy during World War II. And he shared life lessons with me about coaching and leadership. I was truly overwhelmed by the extent of his graciousness and the depth of his wisdom.

One of the things I remember most about our conversation was how much he stressed the importance of thorough and detailed *preparation*. It's a principle I never forgot, and I applied it to every flight that I ever flew from the time I was a rookie pilot on the USS *Abraham Lincoln* until six years later when I was invited back to TOPGUN to be an instructor.

Help Your Team Prepare for Tomorrow's Opportunity

It was at TOPGUN that I saw this principle taken to an entirely new level during my military career. Our mission was to bring the best fighter pilots, weapons officers, and tactical controllers in the United States Navy and Marine Corps to our aviation training center of excellence in the northern Nevada desert and teach them the latest technologies, tactics, and instructional techniques so that they could train others to win in combat.

> The more you sweat in training, the less you bleed in war.

Thorough preparation was the foundation for every TOPGUN mission. Given the extremely complex operating environments in which these aviators would ultimately be expected to succeed, our method was to dial up the intensity during training so that it would hopefully be more like déjà vu in slow motion when the real bullets and missiles started flying. One of our mottos was, "The more you sweat in training, the less you bleed in war."

It was exceptionally rewarding to see those men and women graduate and become instructors themselves, and then watch them train others to perform at such high levels in extremely demanding conditions around the globe. Occasionally, some of them would later thank us for putting them through the wringer, because it helped push them to the next level as an aviator, instructor, and leader. Whenever that happened, I thought of Coach Wooden. I'll be forever grateful for the time and words of wisdom he invested in an impressionable college student who randomly sneaked into his gym one day, and I've always felt privileged by the opportunity to pay it forward.

After John Wooden retired from coaching, people often asked him if he missed coaching UCLA basketball with all of the championships, trophies, and attention that went with it. He always explained that what he missed most were the practices.[16] I'm not surprised. During my time with Coach Wooden, it was clear to me that he believed that's where leaders have the greatest impact—preparing their team for the next opportunity and helping them become the best team they are capable of becoming.

> What am I doing today to help my team prepare for tomorrow's opportunity and reach our full potential?

As a leader, perhaps one of the most important questions you can ask yourself is, "What am I doing today to help my team prepare for tomorrow's opportunity and reach our full potential?" Because while mission success is founded on *prioritization*, it is formed through *preparation*. And finally, it is fueled through the third "P" of mission focus—*passion* for excellence.

Passion for Excellence Fuels Mission Success

One of the most amazing things about the many teams on which I've served or observed over the years is the consistency with which teams rise to the standard that is set for them, provided that the leader of that team holds themselves to an equal or higher standard. On several occasions, I've had direct reports set a standard for their team so high that I didn't think it would be possible for them to achieve it. But almost without exception I was wrong when the leader held themselves to an equal or a higher standard.

As a result, I've come to believe that as leaders we should be setting stretch-goal standards of perfection for our team. At the same time, I realize that's not humanly possible, and we need to learn to accept standards of excellence.

Help Your Team Debrief for Continuous Improvement

So how exactly do you strive for a standard of perfection but embrace a standard of excellence? I think the answer lies in how we handle mistakes. And I think the right answer is to forgive honest mistakes, because honest people will inevitably make honest mistakes. The key is to learn from those mistakes and avoid making the same mistake twice. But how do you do that?

I believe the answer to this question lies in the power of a debrief. I flew over 3,000 flights in my career. Before every flight, we briefed for an hour. Following every flight, we debriefed for at least an hour. At TOPGUN our debriefs were six to eight hours long. I'm not suggesting that you spend six to eight hours debriefing everything you do with your team. But I am recommending that whenever you invest significant time or resources in something, take a few minutes afterward to huddle up and answer three simple questions.

First, *what* happened relative to what you were trying to achieve? Second, *why* did it happen? In other words, do some root cause analysis to determine why you did or didn't accomplish your objective. And third, *how* can you improve as a team next time?

There is one key word noticeably absent from that debriefing checklist. It's the word *who*. One of our primary rules at TOPGUN was to "take the *who* out of the debrief." Because as soon as you put the *who* in it, a debrief quickly devolves into a finger-pointing blame game. And then everyone gets defensive, the "deflector shields" come down, and the learning stops. I'm sure you've been there.

On the contrary, if you focus on *what* happened, *why* it happened, and *how* you can collectively work together as a team to improve, you will foster an atmosphere of teaching and learning that can help take your team to the next level of continuous improvement and mission accomplishment. And ultimately, a team's commitment to continuous improvement is the core of its *passion* for excellence.

Summary

Mission focus boils down to "the three P's." *Prioritization* sets the foundation for mission success. Focus on ruthlessly helping your team keep the main thing the main thing. *Preparation* gives form to mission success. Focus on what you can do today to help your team prepare for tomorrow's opportunity and reach your full potential. And *passion* for excellence fuels mission success. Focus on setting high standards and holding yourself to a higher standard, while constantly looking for ways to improve. If you do these things well, you might reach the moon.

> Focus on ruthlessly helping your team keep the main thing the main thing.

▲ ▲ ▲

As we conclude section 1, take a step back and look at the entire *leadership triad* that we've just unpacked together.

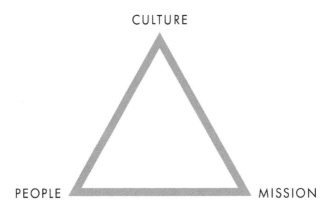

It's pretty simple, really—at least in theory. But the truth is, it's a lot more difficult in practice. At the end of the day, leadership is hard work. However, the difference you can make in the lives of your people and in your team is enormous. The key is ensuring that you are focusing your time and energy in the areas that matter most—your *culture*, your *people*, and your *mission*.

Focus on developing a *culture of trust* by concentrating on your *character*, *competence*, and *composure*. Strive to do the right thing, do things right, and set the right tone. Focus on your *people* by *respecting*, *knowing*, and *taking care* of them. If you do this, they will take care of you by doing whatever it takes to accomplish the mission. And focus on your *mission* by *prioritizing* what matters most, *preparing* for the

> The key is ensuring that you are focusing your time and energy in the areas that matter most— your culture, your people, and your mission.

67

next opportunity, and pursuing that opportunity with a *passion* for excellence.

If you can remain relentlessly focused on your *culture*, *people*, and *mission*, you will create the conditions necessary to help your people reach their full potential and establish the foundation required to lead a high-performing team. In the next section, we'll talk about how to connect these essential focus areas together in a way that creates synergy throughout all three dimensions.

QUESTIONS FOR REFLECTION

- What are your team's top priorities?
- What can you do to better prepare your team for future challenges and opportunities?
- Does your team set high performance standards and conduct regular debriefs to improve?

SECTION II
Connections

In this section we'll expand the basic framework we just built by discussing how to connect the three essential focus areas in the *leadership triad* together in a synergistic way. In chapter 4, you'll learn how to *connect your culture to your mission* through a *leader's intent* that enhances mission accomplishment. In chapter 5, you'll learn how to *connect your people to your mission* by *inspiring* and *empowering* your team members, so they are emotionally invested in your mission and have a sense of ownership for mission success. And in chapter 6, you'll learn how to *connect your people to your culture* by *coaching and developing* your team through effective feedback that inspires your team members to embrace the values, attitudes, behaviors, and standards that define your culture.

CHAPTER 4

CONNECTING CULTURE TO MISSION THROUGH YOUR LEADER'S INTENT

"Leadership is the capacity to translate vision into reality."

—WARREN BENNIS

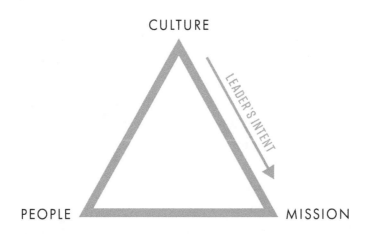

Since the beginning of the twentieth century, the phrase "take a message to Garcia" has been used to describe the importance of showing initiative to complete a difficult mission in the absence of specific instructions. The phrase originated from an essay written by Elbert Hubbard in 1899 titled "A Message to Garcia," which was also the basis for the 1936 film by the same name.[17]

The essay is based on a true story about U.S. Army First Lieutenant Andrew Rowan, who was given a message from President McKinley just prior to the Spanish-American War in 1898. Tensions were rising between America and Spain over Cuba's ongoing struggle for independence from Spanish rule. After the sinking of the USS *Maine* in Havana Harbor, President McKinley felt compelled to cooperate with Cuban insurgent forces.[18]

He needed to get a message to General Calixto Garcia, leader of the Cuban insurgents. Garcia was believed to be in one of Cuba's expansive coastal mountain ranges, but no one knew exactly where.[19]

President McKinley was told there was a West Point graduate named Rowan who could accomplish the mission. The President provided Lieutenant Rowan with context about why the mission was important, then gave him a letter with the simple intent, "Take this message to Garcia."[20]

Four days later, with the letter strapped to his chest, Rowan came ashore in Cuba in a small boat under the cover of darkness. Disappearing into the jungle on foot, he traversed the hostile territory in search of the insurgent leader. Three weeks later, he emerged on the other side of the island, having successfully delivered the message to Garcia.[21]

On induction day at Annapolis, every incoming plebe receives a copy of "A Message to Garcia" along with a 300-page pocket-size manual called *Reef Points,* which they are expected to memorize and apply over the course of their six-week summer indoctrination. The purpose of *Reef Points* is to introduce them to the U.S. Navy's culture by describing its history, customs, traditions, values, and professional standards. The purpose of "A Message to Garcia" is to compliment *Reef Points* by instilling a culture of initiative and a "can do" attitude undergirded by a mission-oriented mindset, even in the absence of specific instructions.

Together they help connect culture to mission by fostering an environment where the use of individual initiative to accomplish the mission described in the leader's intent is both expected and rewarded. President McKinley's intent was clear and concise. In fact, "Take this message to Garcia" is about as concise as it gets. But it provided enough guidance regarding "what" needed to be done within the context of "why" it was important, while leaving enough space for Lieutenant Rowan to use his initiative and best judgment to figure out "how" to accomplish the mission. Clearly describing the "what" and the "why" while leaving the "how" up to your people is the essence of an effective *leader's intent*.

> Clearly describing the "what" and the "why" while leaving the "how" up to your people is the essence of an effective leader's intent.

At the beginning of the previous chapter, I mentioned the concept of a leader's intent in the example regarding prioritization as it relates to mission focus, when I talked about whittling down fifty "requirements" into five core priorities to help our team stay focused on what mattered most. In this chapter we're going to expand on that concept to help you understand how your own leader's intent can help you connect your culture to your mission.

What Is "Leader's Intent"?

Leader's intent is simply high-level guidance for your team that creates directional vision. It can be general or specific. President McKinley's intent for Lieutenant Rowan was individual guidance for a specific situation. However, there are other times when your intent might be expressed as more general guidance that casts a vision for your entire team.

For example, a decade before Apollo 13's "failure is not an option" mission, the United States was falling behind the Soviet Union in the race to space during the early stages of the Cold War. In a televised speech to Congress on May 25, 1961, President John F. Kennedy created directional vision for America with the following intent: "I believe that this nation should commit itself

> Leader's intent is simply high-level guidance for your team that creates directional vision.

to achieving the goal, before this decade is out, of landing a man on the Moon and returning him safely to the Earth. No single space project . . . will be more exciting, or more impressive to mankind,

or more important . . ."[22] With just a few words describing the "what" and "why," President Kennedy cast a vision that unleashed America's innovative initiative, culminating in Neil Armstrong's famous words, "That's one small step for man, one giant leap for mankind" as his foot descended out of Apollo 11's lunar module and touched the moon on July 20, 1969.[23]

Creating Vision and Direction for Your Team

So how can you apply *leader's intent* in your day-to-day leadership responsibilities? Two ways. First, you can apply it when you delegate specific tasks to members of your team, by focusing on the "what" and "why," while empowering them to come up with the "how." By doing this, you'll reinforce a culture of initiative that will enhance mission accomplishment. We'll talk more about this in the next chapter.

Second, you can use it to create vision and provide general guidance for your entire team by giving them a target to shoot for, then empowering your team members to determine the best way to get there within the boundaries of your guidance. By doing this, you'll begin to unleash their innovative initiative, which will propel your team toward your vision. This is what we'll focus on in this chapter.

Unleashing a Culture of Initiative

The concept of leader's intent has its roots in military leadership. As previously noted, new commanding officers typically publish a one-page "philosophy of command" which outlines their vision for the unit. Additionally, a "commander's intent" is an integral part of planning for military operations. In both cases, they provide the person in charge with an opportunity to articulate the "big arrows" that provide high-level organizational direction regarding where the team needs to go and what they need to accomplish, while leaving it up to the team to figure out the details of how to get there.

To be honest, I was both skeptical and reluctant when I wrote my first philosophy of command as a squadron commander. I was skeptical because I wasn't convinced that it would make a meaningful difference. I was reluctant because not only is it hard to synthesize all of your relevant thoughts about leadership into one page, but it also required me to go "on record" about what mattered most to me as a leader. By putting myself "out there" I was now accountable for my words, and that seemed a little intimidating.

But my leader's intent ended up being an extremely powerful and valuable leadership tool. Through it I was able to describe the culture I was striving to create and then connect that culture to our mission by explaining how our values supported our vision. I highly recommend that you write your own leader's intent for your team, because I think you'll find it will help you in four key areas.

Write Out Your Own Leader's Intent

Writing out your own leader's intent will first help you *provide clarity* regarding what's important to you as a leader, which will benefit both you and the members of your team. Second, it will help you *generate alignment* within your team around your organizational goals and objectives. Third, it will help *empower your team members* by articulating "what" needs to be accomplished and "why," while enabling them to use their own initiative to figure out the "how." And fourth, it will *establish the foundation for consistency*, especially when you are faced with challenging leadership decisions.

Soon after I transitioned from the military and started consulting in the private sector, I began working with a team of management consultants to help senior-level corporate executives become better leaders in an environment dominated by volatility, uncertainty, complexity, and ambiguity (VUCA). Based on ideas presented by Warren Bennis and Burt Nanus in their book, *Leaders: The Strategies for Taking Charge*, the U.S. Army first popularized the acronym "VUCA" in 1987 when it was introduced into the U.S. Army War College curriculum.[24]

One of the members of our consulting team happened to be a former U.S. Army Officer and West Point graduate named Ed, who had also co-authored the U.S. Army's leadership manual while serving as an instructor at West Point. One day when our team was brainstorming about tools that could help executives lead more effectively in a VUCA environment, I described the leader's intent concept and explained why I thought it could be valuable. Ed laughed. Attempting to hide my defensiveness, I calmly asked, "What's so funny?" "Oh, I'm not laughing because it's funny," he responded. "I'm laughing because I couldn't agree more. In fact, I even wrote a book about it."

The book is called *The Leader's Compass: A Personal Leadership Philosophy Is Your Key to Success* by my friends and former service academy colleagues Ed Ruggero and Dennis Haley. What is clear to all of us is that a leader's intent is a powerful tool that can help any leader navigate a VUCA environment. And it has been a privilege for me to have had the opportunity to help dozens of leaders across a wide range of endeavors develop and implement their own leader's intent, connect their culture to their mission, and become more effective leaders in the midst of some extremely challenging environments.

What kind of leader do I want to be?

As you develop your leader's intent, it's important to personalize it based on your own style and tailor it to your specific team. Here are some guiding questions to think about:

- What kind of leader do I want to be?
- What is my team's mission?
- What does success look like?
- What are my priorities?
- Do my priorities align with my organization's overall mission?
- What values are important to me?
- What standards will I hold myself and my team accountable to?

I also find that keeping your leader's intent to one page will help keep your team on the same page, so to speak, because it forces you to make it simple, clear, and readable. Synthesizing your personal leadership philosophy into a single page is hard, but I think you'll find both the process and the results very rewarding.

Articulate Your Mission

As we've discussed, one of the key benefits of your leader's intent is an opportunity to help you connect your culture to your mission. As a result, how you articulate your *mission* and the *values* that you will hold yourself and your team accountable to will be extremely important.

In military parlance, *mission* is typically articulated in three parts—task, purpose, and end-state. In other words—what the team needs to accomplish, why it's important, and a description of the conditions that define success (i.e., what mission success looks like).

This three-part structure is the foundation for "mission-type orders" commonly used throughout the U.S. military. It's based on the proven premise that if you tell people what needs to be accomplished, why it's important, and what success looks like . . . you will be amazed by their initiative and ingenuity if you let them figure out the "how." In his book *Start with Why*, Simon Sinek describes how many successful leaders and organizations are using this purpose-driven approach to provide meaning for team members in order to inspire performance and success.[25]

> One of the key benefits of your leader's intent is an opportunity to help you connect your culture to your mission.

Consider Your Core Values

Next, consider your core *values*, which are the heart of your culture. An organization's values are the important beliefs or ideals shared by its members, which serve as broad guidelines in shaping their behaviors, attitudes, and culture.

For example, the United States Marine Corps' core values are honor, courage, and commitment. In the words of General David Berger, the 38th Commandant of the Marine Corps, "These values are at the very heart of our ability to be, 'most ready when the Nation is least ready.' It's honor that gives us an uncompromising sense of personal integrity and accountability; courage that allows us to face any circumstance with an ironclad resolve to do what's right; and commitment that binds us together as a family and drives us toward excellence." [26]

> Consider your core values, which are the heart of your culture.

Connect Your Culture to Your Mission

Once you are clear on your mission and values, it's time to start weaving them into your leader's intent to connect your culture to your mission. Although there is no specific format, a leader's intent commonly contains the following themes: mission, vision, values, goals, priorities, and expectations. I recommend starting with an outline that answers a few key questions:

- Mission: task and purpose

    - Key question: "What does my team need to accomplish, and why?"

- **Vision:** a picture of a future end-state

    - Key question: "What does success look like for my team?"

- **Values:** important beliefs or ideals shared by the members of a group, which serve as broad guidelines in shaping the team's behaviors, attitudes, and culture

    - Key question: "What values will we hold ourselves accountable to?"

- **Goals:** observable and measurable results

    - Key question: "What is my team's primary goal over the next six months?"

- **Priorities:** things that merit the most attention among competing alternatives

    - Key question: "In order to achieve our goal, where will we need to focus our efforts and resources?"

- **Expectations:** standards of conduct and performance

    - Key questions: "What can my team expect from me as a leader, and what do I expect from them?"

Then draft your outline into paragraph form, ensuring that your intent is generally aligned with your organization's overarching mission, values, and goals. You can start by filling in the blanks in the following skeleton, and then flesh it out from there.

"My team's mission is to _____, in order to _____. We will know we are successful when _____. We will hold ourselves

accountable to the following values: _____
_____. Our primary goal over the next
six months is _____. In order to
achieve this goal, we will need to focus our efforts and resources in
the following key areas: _____. As
a leader, my team can expect the following from me: _____
_____. And I expect the
following from my team members: _____
_____."

Examples of Leader's Intent

From the Military World

Earlier I mentioned the first leader's intent (philosophy of command) that I wrote as a squadron commander. I was responsible for 600 Marines and Sailors, and fifty FA-18 aircraft in Marine Fighter Attack Training Squadron 101 (VMFAT-101) based in Miramar, California, near San Diego, from 2004 to 2006. Our mission was to train approximately 100 FA-18 pilots and weapons systems officers for combat every year. I share it in the following paragraphs as an example of a philosophy of command for a military unit and to provide context for what we just discussed with regard to creating a leader's intent.

> It is an honor to serve as your Commanding Officer. I look forward to working with you in the months ahead. VMFAT-101 has a proud tradition of excellence, and I am privileged to serve with you in continuing that legacy.
>
> Our mission in VMFAT-101 is to train FA-18 aircrew for combat. Each one of us plays an essential role in this important

calling for our Nation's defense. I believe there are four corner-stones that are vital to accomplishing this mission: *leadership, communication, professionalism,* and *training.* I challenge each of you to set high standards in these areas and to hold each other, including me, accountable. Be demanding on yourself and others. Never accept mediocrity. Character, integrity, and leadership by example are crucial. We have been assigned the responsibility of shaping the future of Naval Aviation, and we cannot afford to cut corners.

Tactical excellence is our foundation. Fundamentals are our focus. The future depends on our dedication, discipline, and attention to detail today. With that in mind, I ask you to concentrate on three goals when you come to work each day: (1) launching and maintaining quality aircraft, (2) training quality aircrew to be effective in combat, and (3) making VMFAT-101 a better squadron today than it was yesterday. Integral to achieving these goals are the ideals of *teaching, teamwork,* and *service to others.* I expect your individual commitment to these ideals.

People are our priority. It is essential that we take care of our own. VMFAT-101's success depends on the training and welfare of each individual Marine and Sailor in this command. We must invest wholeheartedly in the lives of those we are privileged to lead and serve. We must train, protect, equip, and empower every Marine and Sailor to reach his or her full potential. *We must take care of our people and their families.*

My guidance regarding professional and personal conduct is simple: *Do things right and do the right thing.* Each of you knows in your heart the difference between right and wrong. When in doubt, remember our core values and follow your conscience. We all make mistakes at various times, but as long as they are honest mistakes made in good conscience, they will make us better if we learn from them. However, there are five absolutes I will not tolerate because they will tear apart the fabric of this squadron. They are stealing, lying, illegal drug use, physical or sexual assault, and reckless disregard for procedures that could result in the endangerment of others. We have a responsibility of trust toward each other and the American people. Bottom line . . . be professional and treat others like you want to be treated.

I ask you to consider three things in your daily routine. First, *plan ahead.* Identify potential problems before they become crises. Be proactive rather than reactive. Encourage and reward initiative and innovation at all levels. My door is always open for suggestions on ways to improve the way we do business. Second, *be efficient.* Resist distractions that could detract from our primary mission. We must manage our time and resources wisely in order to properly balance success at work with success in life. Those of you with families have a tremendous responsibility at home. Personal goals, personal relationships, and physical fitness are important, and they require time and commitment. Finally, *have fun and be proud of what you* do. Enthusiasm is contagious, and you have the privilege of working with the most dedicated professionals in the world.

Thank you for your service to your country. You are the best in the world at what you do, and I am extremely proud to serve with you.

When I was discussing prioritization as it relates to mission focus in chapter 3, I mentioned the mission analysis that I conducted when I began drafting my leader's intent prior to transitioning to my final assignment in the Marine Corps as the commanding officer of Marine Aircraft Group 31 (MAG-31) in Beaufort, South Carolina, from 2009 to 2011. I was responsible for 2,500 Marines and Sailors comprising nine squadrons that operated and supported approximately 100 FA-18 aircraft. I also had the privilege of starting up the Department of Defense's first F-35 stealth fighter squadron. Our mission was to be prepared to support combat operations globally.

I share my MAG-31 philosophy of command in the following paragraphs so you can see how my leader's intent evolved over the five years between my time as a new squadron commander and an aircraft group commander. Notably, this one is tailored to a broader mission of operational combat readiness, rather than the pure training mission in VMFAT-101. The operational context surrounding my MAG-31 leader's intent was also different, since by this time we had been engaged in two wars for an extended period of time. My scope of responsibility increased in MAG-31 due to a larger team that was distributed globally. And finally, I tried to incorporate leadership lessons I had learned during my time as a squadron commander, and from my experience in the Pentagon in between.

> It is an honor to serve as your Commanding Officer. I look forward to working with you in the months ahead. MAG-31 has a proud tradition of excellence, and I am privileged to serve with you in continuing that legacy.
>
> Our mission in MAG-31 is to be prepared to win in combat. Each one of us plays an essential role in this important calling. I believe there are four cornerstones that are vital to accomplishing this mission:
>
> - The constant pursuit of *Operational Excellence*
> - Taking care of our *Marines, Sailors, and Families*
> - Protecting and *Preserving our Force*
> - Ensuring our continued lethality by effectively managing the *life and readiness of our FA-18s while we transition to the F-35B*

I challenge each of you to set high standards in these four key areas. Be demanding on yourself and others. Never accept mediocrity. Character, integrity, and leadership by example are crucial. As Marines, we have the responsibility to be ready when our Nation is least ready.

Integral to achieving these goals are five supporting priorities:

- *Aircrew Training*
- *Aircraft Readiness*
- *Maintenance Training*
- *Risk Management*
- *Family Readiness*

Bottom line—winning in combat requires well-trained, tactically proficient aircrew. Aircrew training depends upon our ability to generate sorties with ready aircraft, which in turn requires quality maintenance. Sustained success in these areas requires an underlying foundation of sound judgment and prudent risk management in order to maximize combat preparedness while simultaneously protecting our people and preserving our resources. Finally, all of the above priorities directly depend on the welfare, morale, and esprit of our most valuable assets—each and every Marine, Sailor, government civilian, and family member in MAG-31. It is essential that we take care of our own. We must invest wholeheartedly in the lives of those we are privileged to serve and lead.

My guidance regarding professional and personal conduct is simple: *Do things right and do the right thing, even when no one is watching, both on duty and off duty.* When in doubt, remember our core values and follow your conscience. Because we are human, honest mistakes made in good conscience are inevitable. What's important is that we learn from them, improve, and don't make the same mistakes twice. However, there are six absolutes I cannot tolerate because they will tear apart the core of our ethos: stealing, lying, illegal drug use, physical or sexual assault, child or spousal abuse, and intentional disregard for procedures resulting in the endangerment of others. We have a responsibility to uphold trust toward each other and the American people 24/7. Be professional and treat others like you want to be treated.

Finally, we have been at war for nearly a decade, and will be for the foreseeable future. I am exceptionally grateful for the sacrifices you and your families continue to make which have contributed immeasurably to our success in Iraq, Afghanistan, and around the globe. I also recognize that our operational tempo has taken a significant toll on our warriors and their families. Please create time for your subordinates to balance personal goals with their professional success, and set the example by doing the same yourself. By affording opportunities for our people to balance family, relationships, physical fitness, education, and other personal goals, we will be stronger in the end. Thank you for your service to our country. You are the best in the world at what you do, and I am extremely proud to serve with you.

From the Corporate World

Finally, I'll share an example of a leader's intent from a senior finance director in a biotechnology startup company that I've had the privilege of serving through my leadership consulting work. I share her leader's intent as an example of how it can help connect culture to mission for a corporate team, and how you can turn your outline into paragraph form that can be distributed and discussed with your team members.

I've made the company's name intentionally generic due to privacy and confidentiality considerations. Series B is the second round of investment funding for a startup company. IPO is the acronym for *initial public offering*, referring to the transition of a privately-owned company to one that offers stock for public purchase in a market like the New York Stock Exchange.

Dear Finance Team Member,

Welcome to *Company* Finance. Our mission is to direct *Company's* resource allocation and financing strategy to generate long-term value for patients and investors. We focus on patients first—if we do right by them, returns to investors will follow. We will know we are successful when the company has the ongoing ability to attract funding from the right investors to deliver therapies to patients, and is regarded by investors as an excellent steward of capital.

As fiduciaries of our investors' money, we hold ourselves to the highest ethical standards. We role model responsible financial behavior for *Company* and treat the company's money as if it were our own. We act in service of the business to enable company goals and support the company's culture. We ensure transparency, accuracy, and integrity in our reporting to investors.

This year is pivotal for *Company* as we embark on our next phase of growth. By the end of the year, we will have transitioned to a Series B company and will have laid the groundwork for an IPO. Our primary goals this year are to:

- Ensure we have sufficient capital from the right investors to execute on our next phase of strategy
- Develop a long-range financial plan that lowers the cost of capital over time and a near-term budget/resource plan in line with our strategy
- Establish financial processes and governance to scale the company and prepare for IPO
- Perform the above while maintaining the highest level of financial integrity

To achieve these goals, we will need to focus our efforts and resources in the following key areas:

- Audit and financial statements
- Series B process
- Next year's budget, including instilling a culture of budgetary discipline and responsibility
- Long-range plan
- Finance function scale-up plan and system/process implementation

These are ambitious goals and as an early-stage company focused on scientific research, we will have to work creatively with limited resources to achieve these results. We must do this while maintaining the long-term health of the team, both finance and the company, and well-being of each individual member.

As a leader, you can expect me to focus on enabling your success within *Company*, both in your current role and the next. This includes advocating on your behalf for additional resources when appropriate and being respectful of your need for balance outside work. I will be transparent and open about my objectives and any challenges I am facing, including asking you for help. I am committed to *Company's* success and will work hard to ensure the team's performance.

As a team, I expect you to maintain the highest ethical and performance standards. I expect you to come to me with questions and tell me when you are experiencing roadblocks or challenges managing priorities. I expect you to tell me what your development objectives are and enlist my help in achieving them. I expect you to treat business partners with professionalism and respect to develop trusting relationships.

We all came to *Company* in part to seek out new challenges. I am excited to work with you to build a strong team that can learn from each other to achieve *Company's* goals.

As you can see, this leader's intent is different from the previous two. Although it contains similar themes (mission, vision, values, goals, priorities, and expectations), it is obviously written to a corporate team with a completely different mission focus. Additionally, you can perceive cultural differences through the values and expectations she emphasizes and the tone she uses to convey them. The point is, you can't just copy and paste your leader's intent. It needs to be personalized and customized based on your team's unique mission and the culture you want to connect to that mission.

Sharing Your Leader's Intent

Once you complete your leader's intent draft, share it with people you can trust to provide you candid and quality feedback. This could include selected members of your team, colleagues, and mentors who can provide valuable perspectives to help you refine it. When you are comfortable with the final draft, ask your boss for feedback to ensure you are aligned with their vision.

Then share the final version with your team. If practical, I recommend sharing it via one-on-one discussions so you can answer questions and emphasize or clarify points of interest. If this isn't practical because your team is too large, discuss it one-on-one with each of your direct reports and then circulate it to the rest of your team electronically. Sharing your leader's intent

Sharing your leader's intent with new members joining your team can also be a great way to set the tone early with regard to your culture, mission, and expectations.

with new members joining your team can also be a great way to set the tone early with regard to your culture, mission, and expectations. It can also be an effective way to help you filter potential new hires that you may be interviewing by ensuring that they are aligned with your team's culture and mission.

Take some time to personally review your leader's intent periodically. I found it helpful to review mine every six months. You might want to start by asking for input from your team. They will appreciate the fact that you value their opinion. Then ask yourself a few questions. Are there any lessons learned that you need to incorporate? Is there anything you need to change? Do you need to update your goals or priorities? Has anything occurred that might cause you to adjust your standards or expectations? If so, refine your leader's intent and share the update with your team. If not, stay the course until your next review.

Summary

Your *leader's intent* is a powerful tool that will help you *connect your culture to your mission*. It will provide vision and direction for your team. It will produce clarity regarding what's important to you as a leader, and it will generate alignment within your team around your organizational goals and objectives. It will serve as an internal compass that can help you navigate challenging and uncertain times, ensuring consistency in your decision-making.

Finally, like "A Message to Garcia," your leader's intent will help you instill a culture of initiative that enhances mission accomplishment. It will provide the foundation for inspiring and empowering your team to use their personal initiative, by helping them understand *what* needs to be done and *why*, while leaving the "how" up to them. This is the key to connecting your people to your mission, and that is the subject of our next chapter.

QUESTIONS FOR REFLECTION

- What is your team's purpose, and what are your core values?
- What does mission success look like for your team?
- What kind of leader do you want to be?

CHAPTER 5

CONNECTING PEOPLE TO MISSION BY INSPIRING AND EMPOWERING YOUR TEAM

"Don't tell people how to do things,
tell them what to do and let them
surprise you with their results."

—GEORGE PATTON

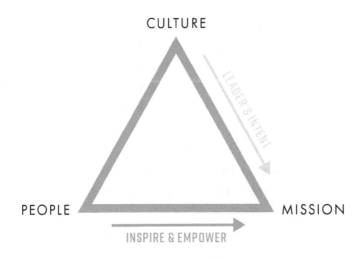

In 1978, Bernie Marcus and Arthur Blank were fired from Handy Dan Home Improvement Centers in Los Angeles over an employee representation issue with Handy Dan's parent company. While discussing their futures at a nearby coffee shop, they envisioned a values-driven company that could help customers create the homes of their dreams. A year later they opened their first two stores in Atlanta. The company was called The Home Depot, and one of their core values was supporting their people.[27]

In their book, *Built from Scratch*, Bernie and Arthur describe how they "inverted" the traditional management pyramid, placing themselves at the bottom and the people working in their stores at the top. Instead of "Corporate Headquarters," the sign at the front entrance to their main office in Atlanta read, "Store Support Center." Their philosophy was that if they took care of the people in their stores, their people would take care of the customers. They believed that the best way to accomplish their mission of helping customers create the homes of their dreams, was to support their people and empower them to succeed.[28]

> How can you take your organization to the next level? By connecting your people to your mission.

Today The Home Depot is the largest home improvement retailer in the world, and is still growing. With more than 400,000 employees in nearly 2,300 stores throughout North America, and a market value of $265B as I write this, Home Depot is currently the 20th most valuable company worldwide.[29]

How can you take your organization to the next level? By connecting your people to your mission. But how do you do that? By inspiring and empowering your team. And how do you do that? Let's unpack those sequentially, starting with how to inspire your team to perform at a high level.

Inspiring Your Team to
Perform at a High Level

The key to *inspiring* the members of your team to perform at a high level is getting them emotionally invested in mission success. I believe this is a two-step process. First, you must generate buy-in to the leader (you). Second, you must generate buy-in to your mission.

Generate Buy-In to the Leader (You)

People buy into a leader when they feel like the leader respects them, knows them, and cares about them. In other words, people need to feel connected to the leader before they will invest meaningful time and energy working toward a challenging goal. Perhaps you've heard the adage, "Leaders touch a heart before they ask for a hand."[30] I think it's sage advice.

> The key to inspiring the members of your team to perform at a high level is getting them emotionally invested in mission success.

You'll know you have been successful generating buy-in to the leader (you) when the people on your team trust you and are committed to the team. In other words, they have confidence in your leadership and are willing to follow your lead. This trust and commitment will stem from you *respecting*, *knowing*, and *taking care* of each and every team member. Trust is a two-way street, but you need to earn it before you can expect it. Earn your people's trust before you expect them to trust your mission.

What is one of the most practical ways to show that you *respect* your people? Take advantage of every opportunity to make sure they know that they are an important and valued member of the team. Two of the most powerful words in the English language are, "thank you." Say them every chance you get.

> Two of the most powerful words in the English language are, "thank you." Say them every chance you get.

What are some practical ways to get to *know* your people? Ask a lot of questions. If you have a small team, schedule regular conversations so you can learn more about their personal and professional aspirations and challenges. If your team is large, focus on knowing your direct reports and coach them on how to know their people (we'll talk more about coaching and developing your people in the next chapter).

But even if your team is large and you focus on knowing your direct reports, get "out and about" (walk around) whenever you can to ask questions and interact with the rest of your team on the front lines. When I "made my rounds" with large teams, I had six simple questions that I liked to ask. The first three questions helped me to establish a personal connection, and the last three helped me learn more about them professionally:

1. *What's your name* (after introducing myself, assuming we were meeting for the first time)?
2. *Where are you from?* I've found that people love to talk about where they are from, and many times there's an instant connection to someplace you've been or someone you know.

3. *Can you tell me about your family?* This is where their eyes usually light up.

4. *What do you love most about your job?* I could typically discern very quickly how inspired they were.

5. *What are your goals?* They were often surprised that I asked. I was often surprised that I could help, if only through a word of encouragement.

6. *What is your biggest challenge?* They were frequently moved that I cared and were usually willing to share. Many times they offered recommended solutions before I could ask, "If you were king for a day, what would you do to fix it?" The more conversations I had with people on the front lines of our organization, the more clearly I could see patterns of problems emerging, along with good recommendations regarding how we could improve.

Carry a notebook with you when you make your rounds, and as soon as practical after you step away from the conversation, summarize the answers and highlight a key point to follow up on the next time you see them. Do your very best to remember and address them by their first name when you meet again. A person's first name is the single most inspiring word to them, and they

A person's first name is the single most inspiring word to them, and they will never forget not only that you remembered their name, but also that you cared enough to remember something important from your previous conversation.

will never forget not only that you remembered their name, but also that you cared enough to remember something important from your previous conversation.

This is a good segue to our third question about how to generate buy-in to the leader (you). How do you *take care* of your people in a practical way? I think it boils down to listening carefully to people's answers to question #6 that we just discussed ("What's your biggest challenge?"), and then doing something about it.

I challenge you to try it, and see what a difference it makes. I call this "the challenge challenge." In other words, I challenge you to ask your people "What is your biggest challenge" . . . and then do something to help them overcome it. I think you will be amazed at how much buy-in this will generate from your people when they begin to know how much you care about their problems. As Theodore Roosevelt once said, "People don't care how much you know, until they know how much you care."[31]

Generate Buy-In to Your Mission

Step two of inspiring your team to perform at a high level is to generate buy-in to your mission. To do this, consider three principles to inspire mission buy-in:

- *Articulate your mission*
- *Reinforce your mission*
- *Illuminate your mission*

You'll know you've been successful in generating buy-in to your mission when the people on your team feel like they are a valuable part of something larger than themselves. Let's unpack these three principles for inspiring your people to buy into your mission.

Articulating your mission starts with your leader's intent. Recall in the previous chapter that *mission* can be articulated in three parts—task (the "what"), purpose (the "why"), and end-state (your *vision* of what success looks like). By connecting your culture to your mission through your leader's intent, you are also setting the cornerstone for connecting your people to your mission by helping them understand their role in the "big picture."

But it can't stop there. Your mission needs to be continuously and positively *reinforced*—like a drumbeat. I've found there are three things you can do to help reinforce your mission: constantly remind your team about the importance of your mission, constantly update them on progress toward your goals, and show appreciation for them as often as possible.

> You'll know you've been successful in generating buy-in to your mission when the people on your team feel like they are a valuable part of something larger than themselves.

First, constantly remind your team about the importance of your mission in order to provide context for their work. I love the story about a tourist who was visiting a city and came upon a construction site where there were three stonemasons at work. He approached the first and asked, "What are you doing?" The man replied, "What does it look like? I am laying stone." The tourist moved on and asked the second stonemason the same question, who offhandedly replied, "I'm constructing a wall." So the tourist walked over to the third stonemason and asked, "What are you doing." The man stood up and smiled, then looked at the sky and enthusiastically replied, "I am building a cathedral."[32] Clearly the third stonemason was inspired by the importance of his mission and was emotionally invested in mission success.

Your mission needs to be continuously and positively reinforced—like a drumbeat.

The second thing you can do to reinforce your mission is constantly update your team on progress toward your goals. Momentum is a compelling force to help keep your team motivated and inspired. Give credit to the team when things go well. Take the blame yourself when things don't go so well, and especially when things go wrong. If you consistently give your team the credit for progress while taking the blame yourself for setbacks, you'll be amazed by the momentum and motivation you can create within your team.

Third, reinforce your mission by showing and sharing appreciation for your people whenever possible. Actively seek opportunities to share these words often with members of your team who are contributing to your mission in exemplary ways.

The final principle for inspiring mission buy-in is to *illuminate* your mission. In their book *Illuminate*, Nancy Duarte and Patti Sanchez highlight four techniques for "illuminating" a vision (remember your vision is the third component of your mission—i.e., what success looks like):[33]

- Speeches
- Stories
- Ceremonies
- Symbols

I had the opportunity both to witness and to practice all four of these techniques during my military career, and I can attest to their effectiveness in helping to inspire teams by "bringing to life" your mission.

One particular example of using a *speech* comes to mind. In the late 1990s I was in an FA-18 squadron deployed to Iwakuni, Japan, to support Korean contingency operations. I had just changed roles from operations officer, where I led a team of ten Marines, to aircraft maintenance officer, where I was responsible for a team of 120 Marines. As a pilot, I didn't know a lot about aircraft maintenance. But my job was to lead the maintenance department in its mission of maintaining aircraft readiness in support of combat preparedness.

Five months earlier we had flown our twelve FA-18s across the Pacific Ocean from our home station in South Carolina. We were planning to fly them back home in a month, when we were replaced by the next squadron in the deployment rotation. But higher headquarters decided to have us swap aircraft with the incoming squadron. We were directed to transfer our aircraft to the replacement squadron upon their arrival in Japan, and we were to take custody of their aircraft when we arrived back in Beaufort.

I immediately saw morale begin to plummet throughout the maintenance department. Aircraft maintainers take tremendous pride in the aircraft they maintain. Over time they learn each aircraft's idiosyncrasies inside and out, and they develop a sense of ownership. Transferring them to another unit en masse was like a punch in the gut. Furthermore, we were in month five of a demanding six-month deployment. Everyone was tired and looking forward to getting home.

We gradually started getting behind on our aircraft transfer inspections, which were a vital part of our turnover process. The rate of maintenance mistakes was increasing. On top of all this, tensions on the Korean peninsula were rising. I had a leadership problem unlike any I'd experienced up to that point, and I wasn't sure what to do.

I decided to put some thoughts together and speak to the whole maintenance department. As a brand-new maintenance officer with little experience and limited credibility, I had no idea how my comments would be received. Nevertheless, I gathered all 120 maintainers together in the hangar around a large map of the Korean peninsula.

I explained some of the factors that, from my perspective, were causing tensions to rise between North and South Korea. I described what role we would play if "the balloon went up," and I discussed where we would operate and what types of missions we would be conducting. Finally, I acknowledged how disappointed everyone felt about the decision to transfer our aircraft to the incoming squadron.

But I also reminded them that the word "Marines" was painted on every jet, regardless of who "owned" it—and that our aircraft would be supporting contingency operations if the balloon went up after we were gone. I thanked everyone for their hard work and dedication to our mission, and then I asked if anyone had any questions.

You could have heard a pin drop. Everyone just stared at me and no one asked a single question. I was sure that I had just failed my first big leadership test and thought that I probably wouldn't last long as the aircraft maintenance officer.

During the next few days, however, I was overwhelmingly surprised. Morale began to rise. Productivity increased. We started getting back on schedule with our aircraft transfer inspections. A few key leaders from the maintenance department pulled me aside to tell me that my "speech" was exactly what everyone needed to refocus and get back on track. One salty gunnery sergeant, whom I least expected to hear anything positive from, even told me that the comment about "Marines" being painted on every jet inspired him to change his attitude. It was an experience I will never forget, because it taught me how important it is to take the time to talk to our people about how they are a valuable part of something larger than themselves.

I've also had the opportunity to learn from personal experience that *stories* are an extremely effective illumination technique. As I mentioned in the previous chapter when I was sharing my first leader's intent example, from 2004 to 2006 I was the commanding officer of an FA-18 training squadron in San Diego. Our mission was to safely train and qualify approximately 100 FA-18 pilots and weapons systems officers per year in the art of basic air-to-ground and air-to-air combat. Nearly two thirds of those aircrew had just received their wings of gold as newly designated Naval Aviators, so we had to transform them from knowing nothing about the FA-18 to being able to fly combat missions in approximately nine months. If we failed in our mission, operational FA-18 squadrons wouldn't have sufficient aircrew for their mission requirements.

Due to this pressure to produce, it was tempting for our squadron to settle in to a "factory mindset." I believed this was a risk to operational excellence, because it could easily create a "Groundhog Day" atmosphere that would catalyze complacency. And complacency is a leading cause of aviation safety mishaps. This safety risk was compounded by the fact that our squadron was in the business of training inexperienced aircrew. Additionally, we operated three times the number of aircraft and flew three times the number of hours, compared to a typical FA-18 squadron.

In order to fight the temptation to succumb to the factory mindset, I tried to use stories to illuminate the vision that I had articulated in my leader's intent, focusing on our mission to train FA-18 aircrew for combat. I made an effort during every squadron formation to tell a story about at least one of the aviators who had recently completed our syllabus and reported to an operational squadron. Many of them joined units conducting combat operations. I made it a point to talk to operational squadron commanders frequently about their aircrew that we had recently trained. To the credit of the talented instructors, aircraft maintainers, and support personnel in our squadron, nearly all of the feedback I received was overwhelmingly positive, and many of the examples about their performance were exceptionally inspiring.

Whenever I shared these stories with our squadron, I could see everyone's eyes light up with pride. The inexperienced aviators that walked our halls just a few months earlier were now on the "pointy end of the spear," making a difference. And that made all the difference in how we approached our mission—with a determined focus on operational excellence each and every day.

Ceremonies are the third illumination technique, and they are a great way to publicly recognize and reward people who are making exemplary contributions to your team's mission. The ceremonies don't have to be elaborate to be effective. In the military we had periodic unit formations where we promoted individuals and handed out various performance awards to people in front of their teammates. These opportunities enabled me to demonstrate how important and valuable they were to our team and provided me the chance to publicly show my appreciation (which helped to reinforce our mission, as we previously discussed).

Depending on the size and location of your team, you might consider occasional gatherings where you hand out awards for employee of the month, salesperson of the quarter, or safety pro of the year, for example. The list could go on, but you get the idea. Bottom line, I've found that recognizing people in front of their peers for their valuable contributions pays immeasurable dividends in the areas of motivation and inspiration among members of your team.

The final illumination technique is the use of *symbols*. Often a picture really is worth a thousand words. Remember my five key priorities in my Marine Aircraft Group 31 leader's intent? Probably not, and I wouldn't expect you to. But if you were a fighter pilot or aircraft maintainer who regularly looked at the five-pointed star (national insignia) painted on the side of every U.S. military aircraft, and if I visually connected it to our five key priorities . . . would it help you remember?

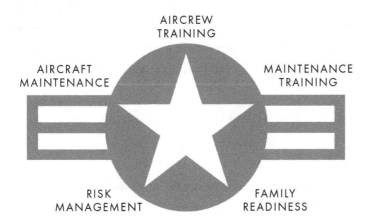

I reviewed this symbol frequently whenever I had the chance to talk to large teams within our Marine aircraft group. I used it to illuminate our mission by reminding everyone what our priorities were and wove in stories to provide examples reinforcing why the priorities were important. I believe it helped us stay focused on what mattered most. And I'll never forget how special it was when one of my squadrons presented me a framed rendition signed by all of their officers and staff noncommissioned officers, which still hangs proudly on my wall at home. Perhaps you can think of a symbol that could help generate mission buy-in for your team.

▲ ▲ ▲

In summary, inspiring your team to perform at a high level involves generating *buy-in to the leader*, and then *buy-in to the mission*. You can generate buy-in to the leader (you) by focusing on *respecting*, *knowing*, and *taking care* of your people—with the goal of earning their trust and commitment to the team. You can generate buy-in to the mission by *articulating*, *reinforcing*, and *illuminating* your mission—with the goal of helping your people see that they are a valuable part of something larger than themselves. If you achieve these two goals, your people will be emotionally invested in mission success. But there is one more level of connecting your people to your mission, and that's through empowerment.

Empowering Your Team to Perform at a High Level

Micromanagement is one of the main reasons why people leave teams. And if they don't leave, it is one of the main causes of underperformance.[34] When people are micromanaged, they feel powerless and purposeless. So how can you *empower* your people and unleash their initiative while giving them a sense of meaning and purpose? By creating a sense of ownership for mission success.

In my experience, connecting your people to your mission by *empowering* them is also a two-step process. First, *involve* your people in creating solutions to your organizational challenges. Then *support* your people in executing those solutions. This implies that you must be willing to push decisions to the lowest practical level and give up some control over the out-come. But I've found that it usually results in a better outcome than you could have otherwise generated alone.

> How can you empower your people and unleash their initiative while giving them a sense of meaning and purpose? By creating a sense of ownership for mission success.

While *inspiring* starts with the team buying into the leader, *empowering* starts with the leader buying into the team. Like we've discussed, trust is a two-way street. The key to empowering your people, and not micromanaging them, is focusing on "what" needs to be accomplished and then trusting them to figure out the "how."

Letting go of the "how" is hard for some people. But as your scope of responsibility as a leader grows, you will eventually get to the point where you can't do it all and control everything. This will force you to trust and empower your people, or else your team's progress will slowly grind to a halt. I wish I would've learned this lesson sooner as a leader. That's why I believe it's never too soon to begin empowering your people.

Involve Your People in Creating Solutions

With regard to the first step in empowering your team, how do you practically *involve* your people in creating solutions to your organizational challenges? I learned the answer to this question when I was transitioning from the role of squadron operations officer to aircraft maintenance officer, which I mentioned earlier.

Not only was this a ten-fold increase in leadership responsibility, but it was also a role in which I had very little background or experience. One thing I did know, however, was that it was important to ensure a sense of ownership and accountability in our aircraft maintenance department. But I wasn't sure how to achieve this, so I reached out to a mentor.

> The key to empowering your people, and not micromanaging them, is focusing on "what" needs to be accomplished and then trusting them to figure out the "how."

"How do you generate a sense of ownership on your team?" I asked.

"Just ask questions," he responded.

"But then everyone will think I don't know the answers," I rebutted.

"Exactly," he replied.

"So what should I ask?" I questioned.

"You'll figure it out," he said confidently.

"Thanks a lot," I responded, unconvinced.

But little did I know at the time that it was some of the best advice I've ever received. Because over time, I learned to ask three "H" questions:

1. Ask for *help*
2. Ask *how* they would do it
3. Ask about potential *hazards* (risks)

I've been amazed to learn that when we are vulnerable enough to ask for *help*, people feel important and they are usually excited to support us. When we take it a step further and ask *how* they would address the challenge or solve the problem, they feel like their opinions are valuable. And when it comes to risk manage-ment, I've found that people closest to the problem have the best instincts regarding what could go wrong. So when we ask them about potential *hazards*, it shows that we have confidence in their experience and perspectives.

When I was a junior leader, I had a tendency to speak first and then ask questions. Perhaps I felt like I needed to somehow demonstrate credibility to compensate for my lack of experience. As time went on, I gradually learned to ask first and speak last. The answers to my questions were almost always better than anything I could have come up with on my own.

Ask first and speak last.

As my scope of responsibility grew as a leader, speaking last in group settings became especially important in order to ensure I didn't stifle honest opinions and productive debate as a result of sharing my own opinions first. By speaking last, I had the best chance of generating ownership on my team. How do you involve and empower your people? *Just ask.*

Support Your People in Executing Solutions

Step two in empowering your people is to *support* them in execut-ing the solutions they created. What are some practical ways to do this? In other words, how do you help your people turn their ideas into action? Consider three "D" principles:

1. *Delegate*
2. *Debrief*
3. *Defend*

SUPPORTING PRINCIPLE #1: DELEGATE

Let's unpack these three principles together, starting with how to effectively *delegate*. In an article titled "To Be a Great Leader, You Have to Learn How to Delegate Well," PricewaterhouseCoopers' Leadership Coaching Center of Excellence Director, Jesse Sostrin, asserts that:

> One of the most difficult transitions for leaders to make is the shift from doing to leading. As a new manager you can get away with holding on to work. Peers and bosses may even admire your willingness to keep "rolling up your sleeves" to execute tactical assignments. But as your responsibilities become more complex, the difference between an effective leader and a super-sized individual contributor with a leader's title is painfully evident. In the short term you may have the stamina to get up earlier, stay later, and out-work the demands you face. But the inverse equation of shrinking resources and increasing demands will eventually catch up to you, and at that point how you involve others sets the ceiling of your leadership impact. The upper limit of what's possible will increase only with each collaborator you empower to contribute their best work to your shared priorities.[35]

I instantly learned this lesson the hard way when I transitioned to squadron command. Up to that point the largest team I'd been responsible for was 120 people. Now I had over 600. It was a huge step, and I had to learn to delegate better. It wasn't easy, but I was forced to improve in this area or risk mission failure.

This begs the question: Why is it sometimes so hard for us to delegate? Some of the most common reasons are:[36]

- It's difficult to "let go" because you like being the "expert" or you just like things done a certain way
- It takes time, effort, and patience to train and develop others and sometimes it's easier to do it yourself

- You may lack trust and confidence in certain members of your team
- You might believe others will resent additional work
- It can simply be challenging to transition from "doer" to "leader" or from "specialist" to "generalist"

One of the reasons why it can be hard to transition from doer to leader is because it's easy to get addicted to your "to do" list. In his book *Leaders Eat Last*, Simon Sinek explains how checking things off of our list releases the highly addictive chemical dopamine in our brain, resulting in an emotionally rewarding sense of accomplishment.[37] In this case, it's important to think strategically about how you are spending your time and what leadership opportunity costs are associated with your "to do" list, regardless of how good the check-offs might make you feel.

> Effective delegation starts with thanking the members of your team for all of their inputs that helped you reach a decision to turn their ideas into action.

On the other end of the emotional spectrum, you might feel guilty delegating something because you don't want to "unload" your work and ask someone else to do something you're not willing to do. Avoid feeling guilty, and learn to embrace the importance of delegation. Two of the main purposes are to improve your organizational productivity and to give your employees step-up opportunities to expand their capabilities.[38]

But maybe you genuinely don't have enough people to whom you can delegate. This is frequently the case with smaller teams or start-up organizations that are growing rapidly. If this applies to you, perhaps it's a good signal that you need to grow your team. If that's not presently possible, then you need to make some tough calls regarding prioritization and time management. We'll talk more about this later in chapter 7.

But first let's talk about *how* to effectively delegate in order to empower your people to execute the solutions they help create. Effective delegation starts with thanking the members of your team for all of their inputs that helped you reach a decision to turn their ideas into action. This will go a long way toward encouraging them to continue sharing their opinions. Then the fundamentals of delegation boil down to clarifying the "4 W's":

1. *Who*—choose the right person to delegate to considering their skills, experience, capacity, and level of interest . . . and your overall level of trust in their judgment and abilities
2. *Why*—explain the context and background behind what you need help with, and why it's important
3. *What*—summarize what needs to be accomplished, and what success looks like
4. *When*—if they are willing and able to help, align on an acceptable timeline that works for both of you, including intermediate milestones and a check-in cadence

To illustrate these delegation fundamentals within the full context of the two-step *empowerment* process, let's assume you lead a team of mid-level managers. Recent customer surveys have rated your team "average" in one of your core functions. Due to an upcoming marketing campaign supporting a new strategic initiative for your company, you want to move the average rating to "exceptional" within the next three months.

You recall that the first step toward empowering your team is to *involve* them in creating the solution to the problem, so you schedule a brainstorming meeting with your managers. During the meeting you explain the problem and ask them for their *help*. You encourage everyone to share ideas on *how* to solve the problem and ask them to think outside the box, emphasizing that there is no such thing as a dumb idea.

Once several ideas are on the table, you ask your team to decouple themselves from their own ideas and consider all of the options objectively. You reemphasize that you are in a psychologically safe space, and you reinforce this assertion through your own tone and behavior. You encourage a healthy debate because you know that for high-consequence decisions surrounded by considerable ambiguity, the most significant predictor of a timely, high-quality decision is the quality of the debate.[39]

The ensuing rigorous debate enables you to narrow the options down to three potential courses of action. You then ask your team members to play devil's advocate to help sharpen the potential solutions by examining both the pros and the cons for each. After zeroing in on two viable choices, you ask your team to identify *hazards* by inquiring, "What could go wrong in each of these scenarios?" Your team discusses risks, prioritizing them according to how likely they are to occur and what the potential impact would be, and then considers ways to mitigate the key hazards.

Up to this point you've asked a lot of questions and resisted the temptation to weigh in too heavily (if at all) with your own opinions, so that you can maximize the inputs and involvement of your team. But now you feel you have enough information to make a good decision about how to solve the problem, so it's time for you to speak.

You start by thanking everyone for their valuable perspectives and opinions, and you encourage them to continue doing so in the future in order to help the team determine the best possible solutions to your problems in a timely manner. You share your decision, and most importantly explain *why* you chose this course of action. You remind them that the two main reasons you are explaining why you chose this solution are so that they will understand the purpose behind its execution, and because one of your primary goals is to help develop them as leaders and decision-makers so they can continue to grow and advance professionally.

You acknowledge that everyone in the meeting might not fully agree with your decision and that they may have arrived at a different solution if they were in your shoes. But you humbly ask for their alignment and support moving forward. You are already thinking about who you can delegate the execution to, but you want to avoid the "boomerang effect" where "no good idea goes unpunished" as a result of you saying, "Thanks for the great idea, Linda. Why don't you take the lead on driving the solution." You realize this approach could keep people from sharing their ideas during the next brainstorming session if they believe there's a good chance they will be tasked with more work if their idea is chosen—so you reiterate your thanks to the team, tell them you will think about who is the best person to lead this, and let them know your door is always open if they have any further ideas or concerns.

That evening you go through the *who-why-what-when* delegation framework in your mind. As you think about *who* you can delegate this effort to, you decide Linda is the best person for a number of reasons. Most importantly, she has the right skills and experience, and you trust her judgment. The next morning you ask her if she has a few minutes to chat one-on-one.

"Linda, I wanted to personally thank you for your valuable inputs during our conversation yesterday that helped our team land on a great solution. I also wanted to reiterate *why* the effort is so important—because it will be critical to the success of our company's strategic initiative. I'd love for you to lead it if you have the interest and capacity, as I think it would be a great opportunity for you to grow professionally and highlight your abilities with our senior leadership. But I also know you have a lot on your plate, and I want to be sensitive to whether this is something you want to tackle right now. What are your thoughts?"

Linda shares that she really wants to lead the effort, but also confesses that this would be adding to an already full plate. So you talk with her about ways to deprioritize one of her current tasks, and also offer to remove one of her responsibilities from her plate for the time being. Then she gets excited about the prospect of leading the effort, so you shift the conversation to a more detailed discussion about *what* needs to be accomplished, and what success looks like.

Finally, you align on *when* the mission needs to be completed. Being careful to avoid the temptation to micromanage, you want to empower Linda to figure out how to best implement the solution that your team created. So you ask her to schedule time with you next week to discuss her plan of action, along with intermediate milestones. You make it clear that you want to empower her to figure out the "how," but also emphasize that you are standing by to support her in every way possible. For starters, you offer to share any lessons learned from your past experience with similar problems, but you are careful to resist the urge to turn your lessons learned into "how" Linda should execute.

To conclude the conversation, you thank Linda for stepping up and let her know how much you are looking forward to working with her on this important effort. And you ask her to think about a good check-in cadence so that you can support her going forward, which brings us to the next step in how to support your people in executing solutions.

SUPPORTING PRINCIPLE #2: DEBRIEF

Delegating is transferring responsibility, but not accountability. Therefore, you will need to supervise progress. This is where the second principle for supporting your people in executing solutions comes into play—periodic *debriefs*, or regular check-ins, that provide opportunities for updates on progress and collaborative problem-solving with the individuals to whom you've delegated.

> Delegating is transferring responsibility, but not accountability.

The frequency of your debriefs should be based on their level of experience and your level of trust in their judgment and abilities. Ask questions and avoid the temptation to dictate or direct. Talk about progress, process, and problems. Discuss resources and risks. Be a collaborative problem-solver with a mentor mindset. Anticipate problems and address them proactively. Be positive and encouraging. Think "coaching and developing"—which we'll discuss in the next chapter.

SUPPORTING PRINCIPLE #3: DEFEND

Third, be prepared to *defend* the people to whom you've delegated by helping to remove any external roadblocks that are identified in your debriefs. Defending the people you've empowered means serving as a buffer between them and upper management when necessary. It involves using your experience and influence to help them remove barriers. It entails actively deprioritizing or depressurizing external demands that threaten their time and ability to focus on the mission. And finally, it includes providing them the resources that are required to accomplish the mission.

▲ ▲ ▲

In conclusion, *empowering* your team to perform at a high level centers on *involving* your people in creating solutions, and then *supporting* your people in executing those solutions to turn their ideas into action. You can involve your people in creating solutions by *asking* for their *help*, asking *how* they would solve the problem, and asking about potential *hazards*. You can support your people in executing solutions by effectively *delegating*, *debriefing* on a recurring basis to help them navigate to the solution, and *defending* them when required. If you involve and support your people effectively, they will have a sense of ownership for mission success.

> Defending the people you've empowered means serving as a buffer between them and upper management when necessary.

Summary

As you can see in the framework on the following page, we've covered a lot of ground in this chapter. I'll close by asking a question related to the opening story about Bernie Marcus's and Arthur Blank's success building The Home Depot from scratch. If your team was asked to choose a descriptive sign to hang over your desk, would it read "Team Headquarters," or "Team Support Center"?

If you focus on the principles in this chapter, it should read the latter. Because when you put it all together, you end up with a team where your people feel *inspired* because they are *emotionally invested in mission success*, and they feel *empowered* because they have a *sense of ownership for that success*. They trust you as the leader and they are committed to the team, because you've earned it based on the way you treat them. They feel like they are a valuable part of something larger than themselves. They believe their opinions and contributions are valued. And they feel supported in executing solutions to achieve your organizational goals. In other words, your people are fully connected to your mission.

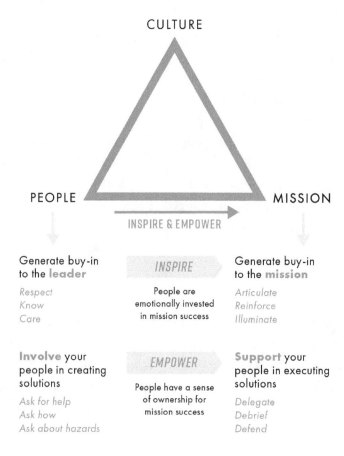

CULTURE

PEOPLE   MISSION

INSPIRE & EMPOWER

Generate buy-in to the **leader**

INSPIRE

Generate buy-in to the **mission**

Respect
Know
Care

People are emotionally invested in mission success

Articulate
Reinforce
Illuminate

Involve your people in creating solutions

EMPOWER

Support your people in executing solutions

Ask for help
Ask how
Ask about hazards

People have a sense of ownership for mission success

Delegate
Debrief
Defend

So far we've connected two legs of the *leadership triad*. In the previous chapter we talked about connecting culture to mission through your leader's intent. In this chapter we discussed connecting people to mission by inspiring and empowering your team. Next we'll examine how to connect people to culture by coaching and developing your team.

QUESTIONS FOR REFLECTION

- Would your people say they are bought into you and your mission?
- Would they say they feel empowered with a sense of ownership for mission success?
- How can you improve at delegating?

CHAPTER 6

CONNECTING PEOPLE TO CULTURE BY COACHING AND DEVELOPING YOUR TEAM

"The mediocre teacher tells. The good teacher explains. The superior teacher demonstrates. The great teacher inspires."

—WILLIAM ARTHUR WARD

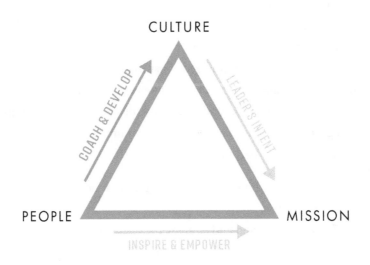

Larry Page and Sergey Brin started Google in a garage near Stanford University in 1998, with the mission "to organize the world's information and make it universally accessible and useful."[40] A decade later they had grown to 20,000 employees in their two-million-square-foot "Googleplex" headquarters in the heart of Silicon Valley.[41]

As the company grew, Google executives began wondering whether the informal culture that Larry and Sergey founded the company on was being threatened by a parallel increase in hierarchy. Eventually they started asking themselves, "Do managers really matter?"[42]

To answer this question, Google embarked on a multiyear research initiative in 2009. It was called *Project Oxygen*, and the goal of the initiative was to eliminate company hierarchy by proving that managers don't matter. The research team analyzed data compiled from Google employee exit surveys, job satisfaction feedback reports, individual and team performance results, promotions, retention and turnover statistics, and numerous training programs. Three years later, the results indicated that managers actually do matter.[43]

Two key findings emerged. First, high-tech employees hate being micromanaged on tech, but like being closely managed in career development. Second, the study identified eight key traits of a good manager. In reverse order from number eight to number one, according to the study, a good manager:[44]

8. Has key technical skills that help him or her advise the team
7. Has clear vision and strategy for the team
6. Helps with career development
5. Is a good communicator—listens and shares information
4. Is productive and results-oriented
3. Expresses interest in and concern for team members' success and personal well-being

2. Empowers the team and does not micromanage

1. Is a good coach

These results prompted a chain of *Harvard Business Review* articles including, "You Can't Be a Great Manager If You're Not a Good Coach."[45] I couldn't agree more. Great leaders know how to coach and develop their people to help them reach their full potential.

Moreover, great leaders know that helping their people reach their full potential is the best way to drive a culture of excellence. Recall in chapter 1 that we defined culture as the collective values, attitudes, and behaviors that characterize an organization. Coaching and developing your team is the key to connecting your people to the values, attitudes, and behaviors that define your culture. When your people are reaching their full potential and your team is pursuing a culture of trust grounded in character, competence, and composure, then the sky is the limit.

The Mindset and Method of a Good Coach

So how do you become a good coach? In my experience, the essence of coaching is *teaching*. I've found that good coaches combine two things well to be good teachers: *mindset* and *method*.

The TEACHER Mindset

First, I believe the *mindset* of a good teacher is one that focuses on *encouraging* people in a way that inspires *courage* and *confidence*. For me, it takes the form of seven attributes that form the acrostic "TEACHER."

- Teachability: do you set the example in being teachable yourself?
- Enthusiasm: do you bring positive energy that is a catalyst for learning?
- Approachability: do you carry yourself in a way that causes others to feel comfortable sharing their challenges with you?
- Credibility: do you know your stuff and lead by example so that people trust and respect your advice?
- Humility: do you admit your mistakes and learn from them, so that others are willing to do the same?
- Empathy: do you put yourself in others' shoes and attempt to see things from their perspective?
- Receptiveness: do you seek to listen and understand before you speak and share your opinions?

MINDSET

An *encouraging* **TEACHER** that inspires *courage* and *confidence*

- **T**EACHABILITY
- **E**NTHUSIASM
- **A**PPROACHABILITY
- **C**REDIBILITY
- **H**UMILITY
- **E**MPATHY
- **R**ECEPTIVENESS

The Coaching Conversation Cycle

Second, the teaching *method* I've found most effective is what I refer to as the *Coaching Conversation Cycle*.

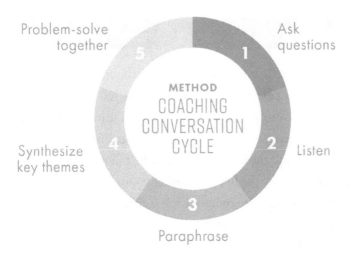

It starts with asking questions in a genuinely curious and compassionate way, and then listening intently to responses. "May I play back to you what I think I've heard you say so I can be sure I fully understand?" can be a good way to transition to paraphrasing the conversation, so you can identify key themes. Finally, once you are aligned in your understanding of the key issues, you can collaboratively problem-solve together with the ultimate goal of helping guide the person you are coaching to their own solution. Collaborative problem-solving will likely generate more questions, which continues the cycle.

In chapter 1, we discussed how *trust* is the center of gravity of a high-performing culture. I've found that success in connecting your people to your culture by coaching and developing them also boils down to *trust*. In my experience, trust in a coaching relationship stems from a combination of being compassionate, candid, and confidential (I call this the "coaching success formula").

COACHING SUCCESS FORMULA

Compassionate + Candid + Confidential = TRUST

If your people believe that you really care about their challenges and growth as a person (compassionate), that you are honest and transparent in your conversations with them (candid), and that what you discuss stays between you and them (confidential)— then you've found the key to unlocking the full potential of your people, and thereby the full potential of your team.

The *Coaching Conversation Cycle* is most effective when it's used in the context of recurring one-on-one sessions. To get the most out of these sessions, block regular time in your schedules. For most busy leaders, if something is not on their calendar, it's not likely to happen. Frequency should depend on the size of your team and the experience of the individual. Avoid last-minute cancellations, show up on time, and put your cell phone away. Being respectful of others' time and providing your undivided attention during one-on-one discussions are critical parts of being an effective leader. Remember that these are extremely valuable opportunities to connect with your people and to help connect your people to your culture.[46]

Preparation for your one-on-one sessions is important. Develop discussion points. You may want to ask your team member to do the same, and then compare lists when you start the session. Plan to be structured but flexible. Begin the discussion on a positive note by sharing a "win" or by complimenting recent work. Use the *Coaching Conversation Cycle* to surface and synthesize issues that you can solve together. Wrap up the discussion by asking about professional development and career goals. This shows that you care about their personal and professional growth and helps keep them inspired and on track. Finally, close the session on a positive note, just like you began. Express gratitude for their work. Words of affirmation are powerful, and, as always, a simple "thank you" goes a long way.[47]

Your Team Needs Regular Feedback

Providing performance feedback will be an integral part of your coaching and development process. Studies show that a culture of feedback at every level is crucial for high-performing companies. Over 80 percent of employees appreciate positive and negative feedback. Forty percent deliberately disengage when they get little or no feedback. And nearly half of highly engaged employees receive feedback at least once per week.[48]

Yet performance feedback can be difficult to provide, can't it? There are some common reasons why. Sometimes we worry that it will cause the recipient to dislike us or cause tension in our relationship. There may have been times in the past when the recipient rejected feedback. Or we may feel that feedback won't help. Fear of an awkward or heated situation might also come into play. The key to overcoming these concerns is remembering that feedback is essential to the health of your organization.[49]

With this in mind, how do you provide effective feedback? Let's answer that question with a series of more specific questions

> Providing performance feedback will be an integral part of your coaching and development process.

to highlight some considerations and techniques that might be helpful.

When and How You Should Give Feedback

When should you provide feedback? When good work merits recognition. When there is an opportunity to improve the recipient's skills. When the recipient is expecting scheduled feedback. Or when a problem can't be ignored because behavior is adversely affecting others.[50]

When should you *not* provide feedback? When you don't have sufficient information about a situation. When the feedback pertains to factors beyond the recipient's control. When the person who needs the feedback seems particularly emotional or volatile. When you feel too rushed to be calm and thorough. When your feedback is based on personal preference rather than a need for improved performance. Or when you have not yet formed a recommended solution regarding the situation.[51]

What about timing and frequency considerations? Provide feedback soon after you observe a negative behavior that warrants discussion, but not necessarily on the spot. Impromptu feedback can sometimes be counterproductive if the giver and recipient are not adequately prepared. When practical, save feedback for regularly scheduled times. As a general rule, give positive feedback in public, and save negative feedback for private. And keep in mind that research has found employees need a 5:1 positive-to-negative feedback ratio in order for them to embrace the negative feedback and improve performance.[52]

How should you provide the feedback? Plan the session. Initiate the discussion with the right tone, focusing on a foundation of trust and an overall mindset of bringing out the best in the person you are coaching. Engage in honest, candid dialogue.

Remember the *Coaching Conversation Cycle*: ask questions, listen, paraphrase, synthesize, and problem-solve together. Express your opinions as personal points of view, rather than unquestionable truths. Pay attention to nonverbal cues, and be aware of your own reactions. Develop an action plan for next steps. Ask them to "play back" the action plan to you in order to ensure alignment. Then set a time to follow up.[53]

How can you ensure that your feedback is effective? Start by having realistic expectations. Some things are easier to influence than others.[54]

EASIER TO INFLUENCE · MORE DIFFICULT TO INFLUENCE

Job skills · Time & work management · Knowledge · Attitudes · Habits · Personality traits

It might be realistic to expect to be able to influence job skills, time and work management, and knowledge. Attitudes and habits are harder to change, but they can still be influenced. Personality traits, on the other hand, are reflections of how we are "wired" (we'll talk about this more in the next chapter). One of the great challenges of leadership is getting people who are wired differently to work together in such a way that the whole is greater than the sum of the individual parts, and where your team is stronger through diversity. So I would submit that this is an area where you could take your coaching to the next level by asking them for *their* feedback regarding ways that you can lead better to help bring out the best in them.

In the end, the effectiveness of your feedback comes down to three questions. Is the relationship professionally positive? Is the process productive? Are results perceptible?[55] If the answers to these three questions are "yes," then you can have confidence that your feedback is effective.

Dealing with Difficult Conversations

Inevitably, some of your feedback will require you to lead difficult conversations. Across a wide range of industries and sectors today in the United States, 70 percent of employees are avoiding difficult conversations with their boss, colleagues, or direct reports.[56] Additionally, 35 percent of managers reportedly would rather jump out of a plane than address a problem with their team.[57] I'm guessing that most of them would prefer to have parachutes . . . but some may not!

> Avoiding difficult conversations reduces productivity, stifles innovation, erodes employee engagement and organizational trust, and destroys teamwork.

Avoiding difficult conversations reduces productivity, stifles innovation, erodes employee engagement and organizational trust, and destroys teamwork.[58] On the other hand, having the courage to engage in difficult conversations can often prevent emerging issues from evolving into major problems.

Some of the most common causes of difficult conversations are conflicting interests, different personal styles (personality type, communication style, work style, life experience, core values), lack of trust, different views of the facts, or strong emotions.[59] Given the fact that difficult conversations are inevitable, how can we best handle them when they arise?

First, consider whether you should have the conversation. Does their short- or long-term success rely on addressing the issue? Is the issue important to the organization's success? Does the situation concern others in such a way that it could escalate if not addressed? If the answer to any of these questions is "yes," then the conversation probably needs to happen.[60]

Next, appropriately prepare for the conversation. Assess the issue and related assumptions from all applicable perspectives. Understand the emotions surrounding the situation. Reflect on your feelings about the issue, and empathize with your mentee's feelings. Consider potential positive outcomes. Focus on your "conversational intelligence," which Judith Glaser, former CEO of Benchmark Communications, describes as the "ability to connect and think innovatively, empathetically, creatively, and strategically with others."[61]

Understanding the Neurochemistry of Difficult Conversations

When preparing for difficult conversations, understand that they can threaten the identity and value of the person to whom you are providing feedback. When our identity or value is threatened, our brain produces higher levels of cortisol. This neurochemical reaction shuts down thinking and activates conflict aversion and self-protection behaviors.[62] I've seen this phenomenon dozens of times during flight debriefs with fighter pilots. And I've felt it myself a number of times as well. I call it the "deflector shield." You attack someone's identity and value in a feedback session, and it's like a protective shield comes down in front of their face to deflect your words. They might pretend to be listening, but they aren't hearing a word you're saying. It's like the owner chastising his dog in Gary Larson's *The Far Side* cartoon, where all the dog hears is, "Blah, blah, blah . . ."

How can we keep deflector shields "up" during feedback sessions to keep two-way conversation flowing, so that our feedback is received and effective? Be as positive as possible. Positive comments in conversations produce oxytocin in our brain, which enhances our ability to communicate, collaborate, and trust others.[63] Remember in chapter 3 when I described how we tried to leave the "who" out of every TOPGUN debrief and focus on what happened, why, and how we can improve? Although I didn't fully understand the neurochemistry behind it at the time, it was all about being as positive and constructive as possible in order to keep deflector shields "up" and maximize learning.

Going a level deeper into the neurochemistry behind providing effective feedback involving a difficult conversation, the top five oxytocin-producing (positive) conversational behaviors are:[64]

1. Empathy and concern for others
2. Being truthful about what's on your mind
3. Stimulating discussion through curiosity and asking questions
4. Painting a picture of shared success
5. Openness to having difficult conversations

And the top five cortisol-producing (negative) conversational behaviors are:

1. Giving the impression that you don't trust the other person's intentions
2. Focusing on convincing others
3. Not being understanding and empathetic
4. Pretending to be listening
5. Allowing emotions to detract from listening

Tying this all together, here are some practical steps for conducting difficult conversations:[65]

- Focus on having a learning conversation—explore, ask questions, and listen (listening can transform a conversation and helps the other person listen to you)
- Set the right tone—ground the conversation up front by acknowledging the other person's value and feelings (show empathy)
- Frame the issue by sharing its impact on you, others, and/ or the organization (decouple this from any perceptions you may have regarding intentions)
- Ask about their intentions (don't assume, since assumptions about intentions are often wrong)
- Focus on issues, not personalities
- Look for common ground
- Reflect before you speak, and paraphrase for clarity
- Problem-solve together
- Be flexible and adjust expectations based on how the conversation evolves
- Agree to next steps and establish a feedback loop

Resolving Conflicts

There is one more point we need to cover with regard to coaching and developing your team. Sometimes your coaching and feedback sessions will surface organizational conflicts that you may not have been aware of. And on the flip side, sometimes organizational conflicts that you become aware of will drive the need for coaching that may involve difficult conversations.

Some of the most common causes of conflict in organizations are personality differences, conflicting values, unclear or overlapping responsibilities, limited resources, poor communication, unrealistic or confusing expectations, or previous conflicts that have been suppressed.[66] Do any of these sound familiar?

Another common cause of conflict is misunderstanding. Misinterpreting communication is often a root cause of misunderstanding, and the method of communication is sometimes a key contributor. For example, e-mails and texts can be easily misinterpreted, whereas phone conversations or video conferences are generally more effective because we can process verbal cues. In-person communications are usually best because they afford us the added benefit of social signals and nonverbal cues. From a biochemical and behavioral science perspective, in-person interactions also generally produce higher levels of oxytocin, which tends to enhance emotional agreement.[67]

> While the quality of our communication can lead to misunderstandings resulting in conflict, the quantity of our communication is equally important.

While the *quality* of our communication can lead to misunderstandings resulting in conflict, the *quantity* of our communication is equally important. Operational speed and pressure tend to reduce opportunities to communicate, which can increase misalignment and conflict. Regular one-on-one coaching sessions with your people are critical to minimizing misunderstandings and misalignment leading to conflict. So make sure you prioritize time for these sessions and maintain a disciplined cadence. Still, conflicts are an inevitable part of leadership.

When and How to Address a Conflict

Before reading any further, think for a minute about a recent, current, or emerging conflict involving one of your team members. When faced with a conflict that involves one of your people, you have three basic options. First, you could choose to do nothing. This might be the preferred course of action if you realize your limited time requires you to choose your battles, and you assess that the situation is relatively low risk. Second, you could address the conflict indirectly by working through a third party. You might choose this approach for a specific issue or situation where you believe the person would be more receptive to feedback from someone else, such as an outside expert or a trusted confidant. Third, you could address it directly during a one-on-one session.[68]

In the context of coaching and developing your people, let's assume you decide to pursue the third option and address the issue directly during a one-on-one session. Depending on the nature of the conflict, these types of conversations can be on the "most difficult" end of the difficult conversation spectrum. What are the keys to success in this situation?

If handled properly, conflict can forge stronger relationships and lead to better outcomes.

First, understand that conflict can be either destructive or constructive. *Destructive* conflict derails projects, damages relationships, and destroys business opportunities. *Constructive* conflict, on the other hand, presents an opportunity to learn and grow.

If handled properly, conflict can forge stronger relationships and lead to better outcomes.[69] Discussion, disagreement, and debate lead to creativity, innovation, and positive change when conducted within a healthy culture where people feel psychologically safe to share their opinions and know that their voices are valued.[70] In fact, there may be times when you want to proactively set up differing ideas on your team in order to generate productive discussion and debate.

Four Main Types of Conflict

Remember that the overarching purpose of your coaching is to help connect your people to your organizational values and standards. With this in mind, consider four main types of conflict:[71]

1. Relationship (personal disagreement or personality clash)
2. Task (disagreement about the intended goal)
3. Process (disagreement about the means of achieving the goal)
4. Status (disagreement or competition around perceived personal contributions or value)

Which category best characterizes the nature of the conflict you're thinking about?

Avoiders and Seekers—Which Are You?

Next, recognize that when it comes to conflict management, most people fall into one of two basic categories—avoiders and seekers. Conflict avoiders tend to prioritize harmony, sometimes at the expense of resolution. Conflict seekers tend to prioritize being right, sometimes at the expense of relationships. How would you assess yourself? It's important to understand your own tendency.[72]

Then, armed with an understanding of the type of conflict and your basic conflict management style, mind your mindset. Ensure a proper time and place to address the issue. Check your ego at the door. Listen and seek to understand the other perspective. And think about the larger organizational context surrounding the issue.[73]

Common Conflict Resolution Techniques

Once you have a basic understanding of the conflict's root causes and implications on the larger organization, consider the best way to resolve it. Some common techniques (both positive and negative) used to resolve organizational conflict are:[74]

- Avoiding (ignoring or choosing not to address the issue)
- Accommodating (allowing or enabling the issue to persist)
- Coercing (responding with threats or other forms of pressure)
- Collaborating (working together to resolve the issue)
- Compromising (making mutual concessions)
- Elevating (raising the issue to higher authority)

Can you guess which techniques are most common?

Research shows that avoiding and compromising are the techniques most commonly used to resolve conflict in organizations. Which leads us to a conflict-handling model developed by Kenneth Thomas and Ralph Kilmann called the "Thomas-Kilmann Conflict Mode Instrument."[75]

Thomas and Kilmann found that a person's tendency toward a certain conflict resolution technique depends on a combination of their levels of assertiveness and cooperativeness. Their research also suggests five core resolution techniques: avoiding, compromising, competing, accommodating, and collaborating (similar to the list of common techniques we previously discussed).

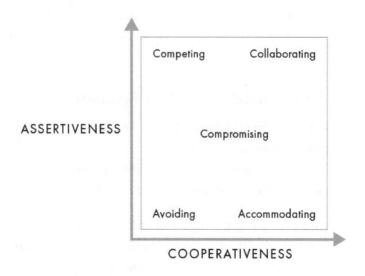

The most common conflict resolution techniques—avoiding and compromising—are the result of being simultaneously unassertive and uncooperative. Competing occurs when someone is very assertive, but uncooperative. Accommodating is the result of someone being very cooperative, but unassertive.

Effective Conflict Resolution

Effective conflict resolution occurs when both parties collaborate and work together to resolve the issue. This requires an intentional combination of assertiveness and cooperativeness with a goal of win-win problem-solving. But we know that this is a lot easier said than done. So what are the keys to being assertively cooperative in a professional and tactful way?

I've found it helpful to focus on what good conflict resolution looks like by asking three questions: Will it satisfy as many interests as possible? Is it fair and reasonable? Will the relationship remain intact? If the answer to all three questions is "yes" then there's a good chance you've collaboratively navigated to a win-win resolution.[76]

If there is one area to watch out for in this process, it's your delivery when presenting a different point of view. It is easy to trigger people into shutting down if we're not careful, and then the collaboration comes to a grinding halt. We've all been there. How can we prevent this? Here are some key considerations:[77]

- Use "I," not "you" ("I feel . . ." or "my interpretation/perspective is . . .")
- Use "and," not "but" (think about how it feels when your boss shares a compliment and then says, "but . . .")
- Use hypothetical "what if" examples to help imagine what it would take to achieve a different outcome
- Use open-ended questions to ask about the impact of a proposed course of action
- Seek to understand the underlying issue
- Admit that you might be missing something, and ask for help understanding

Finally, remember that people are different. One size doesn't fit all when it comes to coaching and developing your team. This is why, as we discussed in chapter 2, it's critical to know your people. You may need to adjust your coaching style based on personality and capability differences.

For example, in his book *Leadership, Management, and Coaching*, James Grinnell discusses three "types" of direct reports—stars, steadies, and strugglers.[78] You might find that you need to be extra creative in how you challenge your stars, and provide them with more autonomy to keep them motivated. Your steadies might need higher doses of vision and purpose in your coaching to help them become stars. And your strugglers may need more attention and direction to help them become valuable contributors to your mission.

But what about "uncoachables"? What if, no matter how hard you try, someone on your team just isn't responding to coaching for whatever reason? The first thing to do is try and determine the reason. Listen and seek to understand why. Ask if there is something you can do differently. Maybe you need to adjust your style. Perhaps you need to change your approach. Or possibly you should ask a colleague to coach them for a while and compare notes. If none of these options work, then it might be time to weigh the pros and cons of having them on your team. At the end of the day, an important part of leadership is understanding that not everyone will be a good fit for your culture.

Summary

Coaching and developing your people is the key to connecting them to the values, attitudes, behaviors, and standards that define your culture. Regular one-on-ones with thoughtful feedback are a powerful way to achieve this. You may need to adjust your coaching style based on the unique personalities and different capabilities among the members of your team. Some of your interactions will involve difficult conversations and conflicts that need to

> By coaching and inspiring your people with the courage and confidence to reach their potential, you foster an environment where excellence is the standard. And when excellence is the standard, the sky is the limit for your team's performance.

be resolved. But if handled constructively, they will make your team stronger.

Although Google's *Project Oxygen* attempted to suck the air out of management, it actually breathed life into the importance of leadership. By coaching and inspiring your people with the courage and confidence to reach their potential, you foster an environment where excellence is the standard. And when excellence is the standard, the sky is the limit for your team's performance.

QUESTIONS FOR REFLECTION

- Do you have regular one-on-ones with your people to help them grow and develop?
- Would they say your feedback feels like valuable, trust-centered coaching?
- How can you improve at resolving conflicts and managing difficult conversations?

SECTION III
Applications

In this section we'll discuss ways to *apply the leadership triad* to maximize your leadership effectiveness. In chapter 7, you'll learn how to *balance your focus among the three essentials* to become a more effective leader. In chapter 8, you'll learn how to effectively *adapt the essentials to lead your team through uncertainty and change* in order to maintain a competitive advantage and manage risk in a rapidly changing operating environment. And in chapter 9, you'll learn how to effectively *leverage the essentials to lead through influence* when you don't necessarily have positional authority, by applying the art and science of persuasion in an authentic way that inspires people with diverse perspectives to work together toward a common goal.

CHAPTER 7

BALANCING THE ESSENTIALS TO MAXIMIZE YOUR LEADERSHIP EFFECTIVENESS

"The most effective way to do it, is to do it."

—AMELIA EARHART

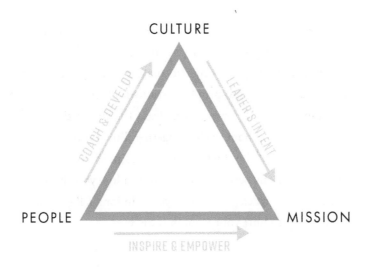

Three-legged stools have been popular throughout history because of their practicality. They require fewer materials, take less time to make, and are solid on uneven surfaces. You might even say they are a physical example of how to efficiently maximize effectiveness.

Imagine a vintage three-legged stool, handcrafted from oak. The thick legs are exceptionally strong. Each leg is carefully fitted into hand-drilled tenon mortise holes in the base of the seat. Since the legs are splayed outward from the seat to create added stability, leg stretchers are used to connect the legs firmly together eight inches from the floor. Because the classic stool was constructed without nails, screws, or glue, it creaks a little when you first sit on it, but it is nonetheless comfortable and solid.[79]

Now imagine that while you are sitting on it, someone kicks loose one of the legs. Or they kick out one of the connecting leg straps. In either case, the stool will lose its balance and so will you. If you don't catch yourself, you're in for a fall, and it will probably hurt.

The leadership framework that we've just built together is like a three-legged stool. It provides a practical way to focus your time and energy in order to maximize your leadership effectiveness. The culture-people-mission triad that we unpacked in section 1 forms the three strong legs. The connections we discussed in section 2 hold the legs together. But if you remove your focus from one of the three essential areas in the *leadership triad* or the connections between them, you can lose your balance as a leader. If you don't catch yourself, you're in for a fall of some sort, and it's likely to hurt your team in some way.

Balancing Tension and Attention in the Leadership Triad

Balanced leadership focus is especially critical within the *leadership triad*. If you fixate only on culture and mission, you could end up with high standards and lofty goals—but no inspired people to achieve them. If you fixate only on culture and people, you could end up with a great environment—but no direction toward a mission. And if you fixate only on people and mission, you could end up with a group of individuals chasing specific goals—but no sense of cohesion through culture.

Furthermore, there are inherent tensions within the triad that require balancing. In my experience, the most pronounced is the constant pull between people and mission. Sometimes taking care of your people can require compromises in mission accomplishment. At other times your mission can demand sacrifices from your people. Bottom line, the best interests of your people are not always completely congruent with the best interests of your mission. So how can you resolve this tension?

The United States Marine Corps has an adage, "Mission First, People Always." This approach has been helpful to me because it's a reminder that we must constantly strive for both. However, when circumstances dictate that we choose one or the other, we should emphasize that there is no "I" in "team" and prioritize mission accomplishment. Recall from chapter 5 that a key component of inspiring our team is articulating, reinforcing, and illuminating our mission so that our people feel like they are part of something larger than themselves. When we ask our people to make personal sacrifices in the interest of mission accomplishment for the greater good of the team, publicly thank them for doing so, and then celebrate the team's success based on the personal sacrifices made, we accentuate this point.

A leader's personality can also create natural tensions between essential focus areas, which tends to draw unbalanced attention toward one area over another. Again, one of the most common examples is the people-mission dimension. If you are naturally wired as a "people person," you might find it more challenging to focus on goals and objectives associated with your mission. Or you might find it challenging to hold people accountable to cultural standards and values, out of concern that it could adversely affect their morale. On the other hand, if you are wired as more of a "task-oriented" person, you might find it easy to remain laser-focused on your mission and to enforce cultural standards but more challenging to stay tuned in to your people.

I can empathize with people who feel this tension, because I lived it and learned it the hard way early in my career as a leader. I was so focused on the mission that I often had little time or regard for people's feelings or emotions. I am ashamed when I look back and think about it. Fortunately, I had mentors like Patrick who helped me understand relatively early how important it is to focus on and take care of our people. And thankfully I eventually realized that it's our people's emotional investment in our mission within an overarching culture of trust that makes all the difference in developing a high-performing team.

> It's our people's emotional investment in our mission within an overarching culture of trust that makes all the difference in developing a high-performing team.

It's important to understand how we are wired so that we can be self-aware of potential blind spots and adjust our leadership focus accordingly. One effective tool to help with this is the Myers-Briggs Type Indicator (MBTI) personality assessment, which is designed to show psychological tendencies in how people view the world and make decisions. It was developed by Katharine Briggs and her daughter Isabel Briggs Myers in the 1940s through research based on Swiss psychiatrist Carl Jung's theory that people engage with their environment using four key psychological domains: introversion vs. extraversion, sensing vs. intuition, thinking vs. feeling, and judging vs. perception.[80] The MBTI is used by more than 10,000 companies, 2,500 colleges and universities, and 200 government agencies in the United States.[81] You can complete an assessment in less than ten minutes, and I highly recommend you check it out (you can find a link to a free version in the appendix).

> It's important to understand how we are wired so that we can be self-aware of potential blind spots and adjust our leadership focus accordingly.

Zooming out and considering tensions related to the *leadership triad* more broadly, leaders sometimes feel strain between leading and building high-performing teams. I actually think the two are complementary, because I believe the essential focus areas are the same. In my experience it takes three basic things to *build a high-performing team*:

1. Attract talent
2. Develop talent
3. Retain talent

The key to *attracting* talent is creating a *culture* that people want to be part of, like a gravitational pull that attracts great people. The key to *developing* talent is creating an environment where those *people* can learn and grow—where leaders respect, know, and take care of their people by serving as empowering mentors who help them reach their personal and professional goals. And the key to *retaining* talent is creating a vision around a *mission* that people are inspired by and want to remain part of.

Prioritization and Time Management Techniques

Due to the inherent tensions and our natural tendencies to fixate on certain parts of the *leadership triad*, maintaining a balanced focus requires disciplined prioritization and time management, especially because there are so many things competing for our time and attention. Pablo Picasso once said, "Art is the elimination of the unnecessary."[82] Similarly, prioritization is an art—because in order to focus on what's most important, we need to filter out what's less important. We talked about the significance of prioritization in chapter 3 as the first important element of mission focus. Here we're going to discuss *how* to prioritize in order to maintain balanced leadership focus.

> Prioritization is an art—because in order to focus on what's most important, we need to filter out what's less important.

I recommend four steps to improve your prioritization and time management:

1. Assess—understand how you *currently* spend your time
2. Aspire—determine how you *want* to spend your time
3. Address—identify what needs to *change*
4. Act—decide *how* to implement desired changes and take appropriate steps

Assess

First, to *assess* how you currently spend your time, you can start with a rough estimate of the average number of hours per day you spend on certain activities during an average work week. I've found the following fifteen categories to be relatively comprehensive across a wide range of industries:

- Sleep
- Food / meals
- Workout / exercise
- Life / personal / home / family / social
- Commute / travel
- Meetings
- E-mail / communication / administration
- Hiring / interviews
- Direct reports
- Boss
- Projects / tasks / research
- Thinking / strategy / reading
- Unplanned issues / opportunities (i.e., "pop-ups")
- Relationships (work-related)
- Other (unique to an individual or industry)

It's common in this initial assessment to be slightly biased toward how you want to spend your time. So if you'd like to go a level deeper, I recommend creating a simple spreadsheet that you can print and carry with you for a week to track in more detail how you are spending your time on an hourly basis (there's an example in the appendix). Each of the above categories begins with a different letter, so you can just write the corresponding letter into each time block on your spreadsheet as your day progresses. Some people like to track their time in fifteen-minute increments to be even more accurate. Either way, I think you may be enlightened by how your detailed analysis differs from your initial assessment.

Then ask yourself, "Where within these activity categories am I focusing on culture, people, and mission?" For example, most of your time spent with your direct reports, much of your time spent on relationships, and some of your time spent on unplanned issues might fall under *people* focus. Hopefully some of your meetings and interactions with your boss, many of your projects and tasks, and most of your time spent on thinking and strategy are related to your *mission*. Activities related to your *culture* might span several categories including communication, interviews, unplanned opportunities, and relationships. Estimate how many hours each work day you are dedicating to these three essential focus areas.

Aspire

Second, have an honest conversation with yourself about how you *aspire* to spend your time. Start by opening the aperture and considering your work-life balance. Also consider your rest, exercise, and diet as they relate to your long-term health. Then determine how much time you'd like to spend each work day focusing on culture, people, and mission.

Address

Third, compare your assessment with your aspiration and *address* any resulting gaps by asking yourself, "What needs to change?" Do you need to shift focus? Or do you need to create more time to focus on a certain area? And what about your work-life balance? Do you need to make an adjustment? And how about your health? Are you taking care of yourself adequately so that you can maximize and sustain your leadership effectiveness?

All of these questions should be filtered through one underlying question: "What *can* I actually change?" I've spent way too much time in leadership positions focusing emotional energy on things beyond my control. Not only did it cause significant frustration, but it also consumed valuable time and energy that could have been spent much better elsewhere on things I actually could change.

> Stop dwelling on what you can't change, and focus on what you can change.

One of the most liberating lessons I eventually learned as a leader was to stop dwelling on what you can't change and focus on what you *can* change. I've shared this lesson with many military and business leaders over the years. More than a few mentioned to me later that this mental shift was professionally game-changing for them. If you find yourself frequently frustrated by things beyond your control, consider the words of A. L. Williams: "All you can do is all you can do."[83] Try to shift your focus to things you *can* control. Both you *and* your team will be much better off.

Act

Finally, take *action* to make changes in your weekly schedule to close the gaps, starting with what's most important. In his book *First Things First*, Stephen Covey popularized the "big rocks" story to help illustrate this point.[84]

The gist of the story is that an expert was speaking to a group of business students on the subject of prioritization and time management. To capture their attention and help emphasize his message, he placed a one-gallon Mason jar on the table in front of him. He then pulled out a dozen fist-sized rocks and carefully placed them into the jar one at a time.

When it was filled to the top with the large rocks, he asked, "Is the jar full?" Everyone in the class nodded their head, "Yes." Then he reached beneath the table and pulled out a bucket of gravel. He dumped some of the gravel into the jar and gently shook it, causing pieces to fill in the crevasses between the rocks, and he repeated this until the jar was "full."

He smiled and asked the group again, "Is the jar full now?" By this time the class was catching on. "Maybe not," one of them answered. "You're right," he replied as he reached under the table and pulled out a bucket of sand. He poured the sand into the jar, and it filled the space between the rocks and gravel. Again he asked, "Is it full now?"

"Probably not," the class responded. Smiling in agreement, he grabbed a pitcher of water and began pouring it into the jar until it was filled to the brim.

Then he looked up at the class and asked, "What's the point of this illustration?" One eager student raised his hand and responded hesitantly, "No matter how full your schedule is, if you try really hard, you can always fit in some more things?"

"Actually," the speaker replied, "the point is that if you don't put the big rocks in first, you'll never get them in at all."

When you take *action* to make changes regarding what goes into your weekly schedule, start with the big rocks. Make sure that your culture, people, and mission are three of those rocks. And then block time each week for concentrated focus on these three essentials.

Taking this action is the hard part, because it requires courage and discipline to let go or say "no" to things we are accustomed to doing in order to make room for what's most important. However, your perseverance will pay off in the form of new habits within your weekly cadence which will help you reach your aspiration. To help turn your prioritization and time management aspirations into reality, consider five potential improvement areas:

1. Mindset
2. Compressibility
3. Task management process
4. Meeting discipline
5. E-mail management principles

MINDSET ACTIONS

First with regard to *mindset*, understand the opportunity cost associated with every activity and try to resist the temptation to feel guilty about eliminating or delegating tasks. Sometimes too many good things can become the enemy of the best thing if we're not careful. And important things can easily be overcome by the "tyranny of the urgent."[85]

Fixation on urgent things can even be fatal to important things. As my scope of responsibility grew as a leader, I often felt the pull to fixate on issues that were generating a lot of external pressure for our organization. Perhaps you've been there as well. It feels like you are getting sucked into a black hole and it can quickly cause you to lose situational awareness to other important things. Sometimes I found out too late that among those other

> Understand the opportunity cost associated with every activity and try to resist the temptation to feel guilty about eliminating or delegating tasks.

things were some bad things waiting to happen, and I could have prevented them had I resisted the urge to fixate.

I should have learned this lesson earlier in my career, because it is similar to flying a fighter mission. The FA-18C/D's RADAR has three basic modes—search, track-while-scan, and single-target-track. Search mode allows you to scan the largest available volume of airspace for enemy aircraft. Single-target-track mode locks onto a single aircraft to provide the most accurate available target information for potential weapons employment, but it is like looking through a soda straw. Track-while-scan is a hybrid of the two modes. Although it doesn't provide the best possible information about a dynamic target aircraft, it produces adequate information for weapons employment while continuing to scan around the target.

> Sometimes too many good things can become the enemy of the best thing if we're not careful.

I could tell you dozens of stories about me getting "killed" in a training flight because I used the single-target-track mode against an adversary aircraft, only to lose situational awareness to another aircraft in the vicinity that eventually sneaked up behind me. As my experience grew, I learned to more effectively use scan and track-while-scan whenever possible. Similarly, as my experience as a leader grew, I learned to avoid fixating on issues in "single-target-track" mode. Whenever you feel yourself getting sucked into a black hole surrounding an issue that presents a risk to your team, stay in track-while-scan. And if the issue isn't a major risk, delegate it to someone who can monitor it for you and provide updates while you continue to search the horizon for the next risk to your organization.

COMPRESSIBILITY ACTIONS

Second, with regard to *compressibility*, ask yourself what tasks you can accomplish more efficiently, and how? Over the years I've found the "80-20 rule" to be fairly accurate—that you can get to an 80 percent solution with 20 percent of the effort, but it takes 80 percent of the effort to get the remaining 20 percent. Admittedly, sometimes the 80 percent solution isn't good enough. But constantly look for areas where 80 percent *is* good enough, considering the value of time. I've generally found that a good solution today is better than a perfect solution tomorrow.

TASK MANAGEMENT ACTIONS

Third, regarding *task management*, think about filtering your tasks into three categories—eliminate it, delegate it, or do it—in that order. Then divide "do its" into urgent versus important. Make sure you purposefully block time on your calendar for important tasks, because if it's not on your calendar it probably won't happen. And as we mentioned earlier, what's important will soon be overcome by the tyranny of the urgent.

> Think about filtering your tasks into three categories—eliminate it, delegate it, or do it—in that order.

MEETING DISCIPLINE ACTIONS

Fourth, let's talk about *meeting discipline*. Research has shown that executive business leaders today spend an average of twenty-three hours per week in meetings, compared to ten hours per week a few decades ago. When you drill down another layer, 71 percent of senior managers across a wide range of industries say that meetings are inefficient and unproductive. Sixty-five percent say meetings prevent them from completing their work and preclude opportunities for strategic thinking. And 62 percent say meetings routinely miss opportunities to improve teamwork.[86] Which begs the question, "Why have meetings?"

It's an important question. I can think of a few good reasons to have meetings. Collaboration, problem-solving, and alignment are at the top of my list (we'll talk about those more in the next two chapters). But the question remains, "If you are going to have a meeting, how can you ensure that it's efficient and effective?"

Consider the following five steps:[87]

1. PREPARE

Start with the purpose. If you can't identify the purpose of the meeting, then you shouldn't have it. Then think through your desired outcomes. Next, put together an agenda that includes a list of topics, the time allocated for each topic, and who will lead the discussion for each topic if applicable. Thoughtfully create a list of attendees based on the topics you plan to cover, and separate them into required versus optional. Finally, send out a calendar invite with plenty of lead time that succinctly outlines the purpose, desired outcomes, and agenda. Put required attendees in the "To" line and optional attendees in the "CC" line, and attach any appropriate read-ahead materials.

> If you can't identify the purpose of the meeting, then you shouldn't have it.

2. LEAD

Start on time, even if everyone isn't on time. Establish ground rules or "rules of engagement" for the meeting. These might include starting and ending on time, asking for everyone's participation and encouraging a healthy debate, agreeing to listen to others and limit interruptions, clarifying how decisions will be made, and establishing a multi-tasking policy. Be the tone-setter and focus on effectively facilitating the discussion by drawing equitably on everyone's perspectives. Stick to the agenda and manage time efficiently. This might involve using a "parking lot" for issues to be discussed and dealt with later. Take notes to record important ideas, key points, and decisions.

3. CLOSE

Focus on concluding with the right tone and clarifying expectations so that attendees are motivated to follow through. Summarize the session. Reiterate key points, decisions, next steps, and who is responsible for what by when. Ask if there are any final questions, comments, or concerns. Finish on a positive note, even if it's as simple as, "Great discussion today, thank you!"

4. FOLLOW UP

Send an e-mail to all of the participants to document the results of the meeting. Start with the date, purpose, agenda, and attendees. Provide a brief summary of key discussion points. Highlight specific outcomes or decisions. Reinforce accountability by listing the agreed-upon next steps, including who is responsible for what by when.

5. ASK FOR FEEDBACK

Request a quick debrief with one or two participants from the meeting. This could be someone whom you respect and trust to give you candid feedback. Or it might be someone who seemed "difficult" during the meeting. In either case, ask for an opportunity to meet one-on-one at their convenience to discuss what you can do to improve the effectiveness of your meetings.

One final consideration for maximizing the efficiency of your meetings is to limit them to thirty minutes whenever practical. Research shows that when traditional one-hour meetings are reduced to thirty minutes, people are less likely to skip them, they are more often on time, they are more likely to come prepared, and they are more focused and attentive.[88] I've worked with a number of teams that have found this to be true, which seems to validate the essence of Parkinson's Law: that meetings expand to fill the time allotted.[89]

E-MAIL MANAGEMENT ACTIONS

Fifth, with regard to *e-mail management* principles, leverage best practices within your team to streamline the amount of time you spend on e-mail communications. One way is to use more face-to-face communications. Recall that in our discussion about knowing your people in chapter 2, I made the assertion that you can't lead effectively from your desk. And in our discussion about coaching and developing your team in chapter 6, we identified misunderstandings caused by misinterpreting e-mail communications as a common cause of conflicts.

But for communications more practically suited for e-mail, there are some best practices that I've found to be helpful. Consider using the subject line to succinctly summarize the topic, and indicate whether action is required or if it's information only. Keep the body of the e-mail as short and to the point as possible, and preface it with a sentence describing your "bottom line up front" (BLUF). Avoid "reply to all" as a general rule to minimize in-box clutter. And develop an efficient filing system that works for you. I've seen leaders spend an exorbitant amount of time filing e-mails categorically, when it would be far more efficient to file them in chronological folders (e.g., by calendar year depending on file size for backup considerations), then use the search feature to recall them if needed. And immediately after you read an e-mail (and respond, if appropriate), you should do one of three things: file it in your chronological folder, move it to a "follow-up" folder or electronic "to do" list which you review periodically, or delete it.

Finally, it can be helpful to establish team norms for expected e-mail response times. This way, if the expectation is that team members will respond within twenty-four hours, for example, and you haven't received a response within that timeframe, you can reach out to the team member through other means. If you receive an e-mail from a team member and are unable to adequately respond within the agreed-upon timeframe, you can reply with a quick note to let them know you received it and will respond as soon as practical.

Summary

All of these prioritization and time management techniques are simply a means to help you maintain balanced focus on your team's *culture*, *people*, and *mission*. At the beginning of this chapter we discussed organizational tensions and leadership tendencies that can threaten this balance. The art of balancing these tensions and tendencies related to the *leadership triad* is the key to maximizing your leadership effectiveness. Mastering this equilibrium will enable you to build and lead a high-performing team. But this equilibrium cannot remain static if you want to *sustain* a high-performing team. It must be dynamic, because tomorrow is changing more rapidly than ever—and that is the topic of our next chapter.

QUESTIONS FOR REFLECTION

- Where do you find the most tension in the leadership triad?
- What do you need to prioritize to become a better, more balanced leader?
- What do you need to change in order to manage your time better?

CHAPTER 8

ADAPTING THE ESSENTIALS TO LEAD THROUGH UNCERTAINTY AND CHANGE

"The future ain't what it used to be."

—YOGI BERRA

Technological change is accelerating exponentially. Innovations in the fields of artificial intelligence, robotics, 3D printing, autonomous vehicles, augmented reality, nanotechnology, and genetic engineering, just to name a few, are expanding the frontiers of what we previously thought was possible. Enabling the speed of innovation are advances in information technology, which are expanding the boundaries of what we previously thought was knowable.[90]

Ninety percent of the data in the world today was created in the last two years. Moreover, the size of the digital universe continues to double every two years.[91] You have access to more information on your cell phone than previous generations could accumulate in a lifetime. Yet the ability to convert the vast volume and velocity of today's information flow into actionable knowledge seems more challenging than ever.

The magnitude and rate of change in today's world are driving unprecedented levels of complexity and uncertainty into organizational operating environments. As a result, one of the most important questions leaders of high-performing teams must ask themselves is, "How can we develop the agility required to maintain a competitive advantage in the face of such rapidly changing complexity and uncertainty?"

Leading Through Uncertainty

When I take a step back and think about the nature of uncertainty, I find it amusing to consider the perspectives of three successful leaders in recent history who had very different backgrounds and opinions on the topic. Yogi Berra, All-Star catcher for the New York Yankees from 1946–1963 and one of America's most beloved "philosophers," famously stated, "It's tough to make predictions, especially about the future" and "When you come to a fork in the road, take it."[92] Alan Kay, who was an Advanced Technology Group Fellow with Apple from 1984 to 1997 said, "The best way to predict the future is to invent it."[93] And General Dwight D. Eisenhower often said that, "Plans are worthless, but planning is everything.[94]

As the architect of one of the most complex and successful military operations in history—the invasion of Normandy (codenamed "Operation Overlord") on "D-Day" during World War II, which resulted in the eventual defeat of Hitler's Nazi German regime—General Eisenhower was intimately familiar with the military adage that, "No plan survives contact with the enemy," because the enemy gets a vote.[95] But he also knew

> Collaborative planning is the foundation for agility.

that *collaborative planning* is the foundation for *agility*, because it creates a common operating baseline in a shared information environment that enables rapid adjustments during changing circumstances in order to maintain a competitive advantage.

In 1997, building on General Eisenhower's lessons about collaborative planning, the U.S. Army developed its current seven-step *Military Decision-Making Process*.[96] It was designed to respond to the "VUCA" (volatility, uncertainty, complexity, and ambiguity) environment that we discussed in chapter 4, and its purpose is to help teams plan for success in exceptionally dynamic environments.

Using the Collaborative Planning Process to Help Your Team

I've had the opportunity to share an adaptation of the Military Decision-Making Process with leaders and teams operating in VUCA environments across a wide range of industries outside the military. Because it has proven valuable to many of them, I want to share it with you. I call it the *Collaborative Planning Process,* and I believe it can be a valuable tool in your leadership toolbox to help you sharpen your focus when your team is challenged with high degrees of uncertainty. The process contains seven steps, which we'll unpack together in the pages ahead.

1. LEADER'S GUIDANCE

The first step involves you providing your high-level *leader's guidance* to your team. Think about this in terms of the mission you need to accomplish. Then define the mission clearly and succinctly in three parts: (1) what needs to be accomplished (i.e., the *task*), (2) why it's important (i.e., the *purpose*), and (3) what success looks like (i.e., the desired *end-state*).

For example, let's say your team has been on the leading edge of developing and delivering a new service for your company to

COLLABORATIVE PLANNING PROCESS

STEP	DESCRIPTION
1. LEADER'S GUIDANCE	Mission: *What, Why, Success Criteria* (Task, Purpose, End-state)
2. MISSION ANALYSIS	Planning factors: "CRAFT" • *Competition, Resources, Atmospherics (e.g., social, cultural, political, regulatory), Functions (expertise needed for planning and execution), Time*
3. COA DEVELOPMENT	Course of Action (COA): *What needs to be done, by When, by Whom* • *Cross-functional, task-organized team*
4. CONTINGENCY PLANNING	• What could go wrong (risks)? What could go unexpectedly well (opportunities)? • How will you know that these risks/opportunities are developing (critical information triggers)? • What will you do about them (contingency responses)?
5. DECISION	• At least two COAs for the decision-maker to choose from (or combine) • Brief the Mission Analysis, COA overview, key contingency plans, pros/cons assessment
6. EXECUTION	Clearly communicate initially to the execution team, and iteratively as required: • *Leader's Guidance, Mission Analysis (mission and context)* • *Execution team roles and responsibilities (who does what when, contingency responses)*
7. DEBRIEF	Focus on continuous improvement for the planning and execution team(s) • *Performance (results vs. objectives)* • *Process*

customers in a certain business sector. Because of your success, most of your team's work is now concentrated in this area. Your company's senior leadership just completed a strategy review suggesting that based on current economic trends, this sector is ripe for a disruption that could deal a blow to your financial bottom line and force your team to downsize. You don't know if or when this will happen, but you want to explore options for diversifying in order to manage the risk of a disruption and maintain a competitive advantage for your team.

You spend some time developing your high-level leader's guidance. Then you get your team together to share it with them. Starting with the background, you explain, "Team, senior leadership just finished a strategy review that shows we may be over-concentrating services and resources in our sector. This creates a risk for us, because if there is a future disruption, which is likely, it could force us to downsize. So I need your help."

Then you shift to articulating the *mission*, beginning with the *task* and *purpose*. "We need to diversify our services into other areas in order to manage the risk of a potential disruption in our sector." And finally, you paint a picture of the *end-state*. "If we are successful, within twelve months we will be serving a portfolio of different sectors with the same commitment to excellence that got us where we are today, and we will be poised for sustained growth over time despite a potential downturn in any individual sector."

Next you select a subset of your team to form a *Collaborative Planning Team* (CPT) and empower them to tackle the issue. You might start with volunteers. Ultimately though, you need to ensure that the right people are in the room so that the CPT has adequate expertise to consider all likely facets of the solution. Now that you've clearly defined the "what" and identified your planning team, it's time for you to step away and let them get to work developing options that they can present to you later regarding the "how." Before you go, you remind them of three things that will be critical in generating the best answer: collecting all of the relevant data and facts, encouraging rigorous debate, and remaining tuned in to the strategic context.

2. MISSION ANALYSIS

Your CPT then launches into step two—*mission analysis*. As a group they discuss and analyze what factors could affect the mission. They craft their assessment using the acrostic "CRAFT" to consider *competition*, available *resources*, *atmospherics* (e.g., social, cultural, political, regulatory, etc.), additional *functions* (i.e., expertise) you might need as you pursue your objective, and *time* factors, plus any other unique considerations that could impact mission accomplishment.

Mission analysis is the most commonly overlooked step in effective planning. Most of us want to jump right to solutions. However, if you don't fully understand important aspects of your mission, you are likely to arrive at a solution that misses the mark. In other words, as Yogi Berra once said, "You've got to be very careful if you don't know where you are going, because you might not get there."[97]

3. COURSE OF ACTION (COA) DEVELOPMENT

Once your team has a grasp of the key aspects of your mission, they move to step three—*COA development*. In order to push the depth and breadth of their thinking, you've asked them to develop three separate COAs that are feasible and distinguishable, meaning that they are all practically doable and different.

Your planning team begins by brainstorming to identify three high-level concepts of operation that are all feasible and distinguishable. Next, for each COA they break down the concept of operation into discrete steps. Then, for each step they define "who does what when." This forms the basis for a cross-functional, task-organized team that would be required to execute the COA.

4. CONTINGENCY PLANNING

Since your team has heard you occasionally remind them, "No plan survives contact with customers, competition, or chance," they now turn their focus to step four—*contingency planning*. For each COA they ask each other, "What could go wrong?" in order to capture a list of key risks. Next they ask, "What could go unexpectedly well?" and then create a list of potential opportunities. Then they cluster similar answers into themes and plot them on a simple four-quadrant graph like the one below.

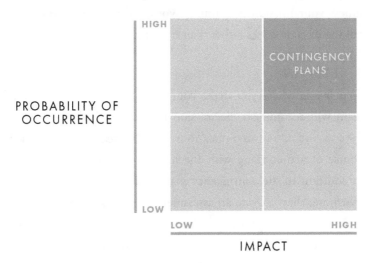

For each risk and opportunity that lands in the top right quadrant (high probability of occurrence and high impact), the CPT develops a contingency plan. Each plan answers two questions. First, "How will we know if the risk or opportunity is developing?" In other words, what critical information will you need, and how will you get it? The second question is, "What will we do about it?" That is, what steps will form your contingency response to mitigate the risk or capitalize on the opportunity?

Now it's time for your *Collaborative Planning Team* to brief you on their mission analysis, courses of action, and contingency plans so that you can make a decision on how to move forward. How long should this process take up until this point? It depends on the complexity of the challenge, the urgency of the issue, and the bandwidth of your team. To put this into perspective, it took General Eisenhower and his staff six months to plan Operation Overlord.[98] Granted, he had a large staff and a sense of urgency driven by the future of the free world hanging in the balance, but the challenge was also enormously complex. As a rule of thumb, unless your mission is winning World War III, we're probably talking days or weeks rather than months.

5. DECISION

Step five is where you make your *decision* regarding how your team will accomplish the mission that you articulated in your *leader's guidance* in step one. Your planning team describes each course of action along with the mission analysis behind them, in addition to the contingency plans associated with each. Furthermore, they provide an assessment of pros and cons for each COA. You are impressed by the innovative thinking, creativity, and rigor behind each option. You ask questions throughout each brief to help clarify key considerations. The team's answers clearly indicate that they have done their homework and considered each option from all relevant angles. Now it's time for you to make a decision. But how do you decide?

Effective decision-making boils down to judgment. In a *Harvard Business Review* article titled "The Elements of Good Judgment," Andrew Likierman describes six components of good judgment: learning, trust, experience, detachment, options, and delivery. With respect to *learning*, leaders with good judgment tend to be good readers and listeners. Regarding *trust*, they intentionally draw on the diverse perspectives and experiences of others. They combine these factors with their own *experience*, and try to *detach* themselves emotionally from the issue in order to minimize bias. They question aspects of the *options* being offered, and finally factor in the feasibility of being able to *deliver* on the decision.[99]

Most of these elements are already baked into the *Collaborative Planning Process*, including asking your planning team to develop feasible and distinguishable COAs, drawing on diverse perspectives and expertise to develop them, and carefully listening to your team explain each COA while leveraging your own personal and professional experience (which has probably been honed through reading) to ask clarifying questions. If you can also listen objectively and minimize any personal bias, then you've got them all covered.

But what if you've done all of this and the right decision still isn't clear to you? Making good decisions in an environment of complexity and ambiguity is one of the main reasons why leadership is so hard. When you find yourself in this situation, I've found it helpful to run the decision through four filters: ask probing questions, ask yourself three key questions, trust your instinct, and verify the logic.

Decision Filter #1: Ask Probing Questions. The first filter is asking tough, pointed questions until the right decision becomes clear. Often the complexity and ambiguity surrounding a difficult decision is caused by not having an integrated, fused picture of what is really going on. If you are not getting clear, confident answers from your team, keep probing until you do. You don't need to be a jerk about it, but you do need to be persistent. "I'm sorry to be such a pain, but help me understand . . ." can be an effective way to soften the questions. Many times an answer to one of your probing questions will eventually cause the light bulb to come on and you'll have one of those, "Ahh, now I get it, thank you" moments which will be the key for your decision.

But sometimes the light bulb still doesn't come on, no matter how many questions you ask. I can tell you from personal experience that some of the worst decisions I made in my military career were a result of moving forward with a decision without being fully satisfied with the answers I was getting from my team. It takes courage and conviction to keep probing when it feels like there is something missing from the answers you are getting, but you can't put your finger on it and you don't want to be perceived as a jerk. Sadly, the times I felt like that and failed to persevere with tough questions almost always resulted in tougher challenges and deeper problems for our organization down the road.

Decision Filter #2: Ask Yourself Three Key Questions. When the light bulb doesn't come on through the first filter of tough questions for your team, then what? I've found it helpful to run the decision through a second filter of three key questions for yourself: "Will this decision help accomplish our mission?" "Will it help take care of our people?" "And will it uphold our organizational values?" In other words, will it support your culture, people, and mission? If the answer to all three questions is "yes," then I've almost always found it to be a good decision.

Decision Filter #3: Trust Your Instinct. But what if you are in the fortunate position of having to make a decision involving multiple options where the answer to all three questions is "yes" for all of the options? Then I recommend using a third filter, which is sometimes referred to as "rule number one of leadership"—*trust your instinct*.

In his *New York Times* best-selling book, *Thinking Fast and Slow*, Nobel Prize–winning author Daniel Kahneman describes how our intuition (the "fast thinking" part of our brain) can sometimes be more accurate than the logical and deliberate "slow thinking" part of our brain when it comes to judgment and decision-making. Many times this is a result of experience. Other times it's that our unconscious mind can recognize patterns more quickly and accurately than through conscious calculations and reasoning. His main point is that these two parts or "systems" of our thinking, instinct and logic, work together to help us make decisions, and we should not underestimate the power of our "gut."[100]

Decision Filter #4: Verify the Logic. During his nuclear disarmament discussions with the Soviet Union leading up to the signing of the Intermediate-Range Nuclear Forces Treaty in 1987, Ronald Reagan often used the phrase, "Trust, but verify."[101] I think of this as the fourth filter for effective decision-making. Since our minds use both instinct and logic to make decisions, trust your instinct but verify it with logic.

To do this, I like to go through a deliberate decision-making checklist that I've developed over the years:

1. Is this a decision that I need to make now? Check.
2. Did I consider the strategic context, including realistic constraints? Check.
3. Did I get the right people with the right expertise in the room? Check.
4. Did I accurately frame the issue and encourage rigorous debate? Check.
5. Did I collect all of the relevant facts and consider all aspects of the issue? Check.
6. Did I identify and appropriately weigh the risks and opportunities? Check.
7. Do I feel enough conviction to be decisive and explain *why* I made the decision? Let's talk more about this one.

As a quick review of where we are in the *Collaborative Planning Process*, recall from our example that your team's services and resources are too concentrated in a particular sector, and you need to diversify into other areas in order to manage the risk of a potential disruption. In step one you issued your *leader's guidance* to your planning team. In step two they conducted their *mission analysis*, and then in step three they developed three feasible and distinguishable *courses of action*. In step four your team developed *contingency plans* to address risks and opportunities associated with each course of action. And now in step five, you need to make a *decision*.

You've applied your best judgment and have run your decision through the four filters we just discussed, but you still don't feel enough conviction to be decisive about any one of the three courses of action your team has presented. You've logically narrowed your decision down to COAs #1 and #3. But your instinct is that you like elements of each option. So you choose to

COLLABORATIVE PLANNING PROCESS

STEP	DESCRIPTION
1. LEADER'S GUIDANCE	Mission: *What, Why, Success Criteria* (Task, Purpose, End-state)
2. MISSION ANALYSIS	Planning factors: "CRAFT" • *Competition, Resources, Atmospherics (e.g., social, cultural, political, regulatory), Functions (expertise needed for planning and execution), Time*
3. COA DEVELOPMENT	Course of Action (COA): *What* needs to be done, by *When*, by *Whom* • *Cross-functional, task-organized team*
4. CONTINGENCY PLANNING	• What could go wrong (risks)? What could go unexpectedly well (opportunities)? • How will you know that these risks/opportunities are developing (critical information triggers)? • What will you do about them (contingency responses)?
5. DECISION	• At least two COAs for the decision-maker to choose from (or combine) • Brief the Mission Analysis, COA overview, key contingency plans, pros/cons assessment
6. EXECUTION	Clearly communicate initially to the execution team, and iteratively as required: • *Leader's Guidance, Mission Analysis (mission and context)* • *Execution team roles and responsibilities (who does what when, contingency responses)*
7. DEBRIEF	Focus on continuous improvement for the planning and execution team(s) • *Performance (results vs. objectives)* • *Process*

combine those elements into a "hybrid" COA comprising what you believe are the best of each.

Now, both your heart and your mind are convinced that this is the best decision. You finally feel enough conviction to be decisive and explain *why* you made the decision. In order to help your team understand your thought process and the purpose behind your decision, you explain to them *why* you reached this conclusion. Then you ask your team to consolidate these hybrid elements into "the" plan, and now it's time to execute.

6. EXECUTION

Step six is *executing* your plan. This starts with confirming who needs to be on your execution team. Often it's the CPT members, since they were originally chosen based on their functional expertise, and they have the most situational awareness of the plan because they developed and analyzed it. But it doesn't have to be. In the course of their collaborative planning, your team may have identified others who would be better suited for the execution team, based on their functional expertise. Or perhaps you might choose different members based on geographical considerations. At a minimum, the execution team needs to include all of the individuals in the COA steps that define "who does what when," in addition to the people who will be involved in executing potential contingency plans.

The key to successful execution is ensuring that it is decentralized, meaning each member of the team is empowered to perform their role and make real-time adjustments based on rapidly evolving conditions throughout your shared information environment. This requires each member of your execution team to clearly understand the plan and their role in it. A lack of clearly defined and understood roles and responsibilities is the most common cause of mission failure. Clear, deliberate, and consistent communications throughout execution are the best way to avoid this, especially when conditions are rapidly changing.

7. DEBRIEF

The seventh and final step is to *debrief* your planning and execution. We discussed the power of debriefing in chapter 3 when we talked about the concept of passion for excellence as it relates to mission focus. The point is that debriefs should concentrate on continuous improvement. Depending on the length of time in your execution window, you might want to debrief regularly throughout. Whatever frequency you decide, start every debrief by admitting your own mistakes as the leader. You'll be amazed by how this will inspire the members of your team to acknowledge their mistakes. Focus on both planning and execution. Evaluate both process and performance. Measure objectives versus outcomes. Remember the three key debrief questions—what happened, why, and how can we improve next time? Leave the "who" out of it. Finally, capture and codify lessons learned for continuous improvement.

> Start every debrief by admitting your own mistakes as the leader.

In my experience, the *Collaborative Planning Process* can be an extremely effective tool to help you lead your team through uncertainty by creating a common operating baseline in a shared information environment that can enable rapid adjustments during changing circumstances to maintain a competitive advantage. But to implement it effectively, remember the adage that "no plan survives contact," because others (customers, competition, chance, etc.) each get a vote. As a result, you must embrace the inevitability that operational changes will be required to successfully navigate toward your objective.

Leading Operational Change

Some operational changes can be anticipated through *contingency planning* like we just discussed in step four of the *Collaborative Planning Process*. But since none of us has a crystal ball and it's impossible to proactively anticipate every problem that could occur, it is also helpful to have a rapid process for reactive problem-solving. I've found the following process helpful in these situations.[102]

Using the Problem-Solving Process to Help Your Team

PROBLEM-SOLVING PROCESS

STEP	DESCRIPTION	COMMENTS
1	DEFINE THE PROBLEM	Clearly articulate and align on the answer to, "What problem are we trying to solve?"
2	DISSECT THE PROBLEM	Identify the key issues
3	PRIORITIZE KEY ISSUES	Which questions are most critical, and which ones are likely less important?
4	PLAN YOUR RESEARCH	Think efficiency (time and resources)
5	CONDUCT RESEARCH & ANALYSIS	Think 80-20 rule
6	SYNTHESIZE YOUR FINDINGS	What is the "so what"? (i.e., what practical actions are implied by the findings)
7	PROPOSE YOUR SOLUTION	Answer to the question, "What should we do?" (think clarity and impact)

1. DEFINE THE PROBLEM

The first step is to define the problem and make sure your problem-solving team is fully aligned on the answer to the question, "What problem are we trying to solve?" You should be able to articulate this clearly and succinctly.

2. DISSECT THE PROBLEM

Step two is to dissect the problem into potential root causes so that you can identify the key issues. One way to "pull the problem apart" is to create an "issue tree." You can do this by writing your problem statement on the left side of a whiteboard, and then create branches from left to right identifying root issues, and then sub issues, etc.

3. PRIORITIZE KEY ISSUES

Once you've identified the key issues, step three is to prioritize them. Ask yourself, "Which issues seem most critical, and what questions do we need to answer in order to run these issues to ground?"

4. PLAN YOUR RESEARCH

Step four is to plan your research in order to answer the critical questions identified in step three. Consider the amount of time and resources you have available, and develop a plan that focuses on efficiency.

5. CONDUCT RESEARCH AND ANALYSIS

Step five is to do the research that you've just planned and analyze what you find. Maybe your team can divide and conquer, and then assemble to discuss findings. Whatever you do, remember the 80-20 rule that we discussed in the previous chapter regarding prioritization, and strive for the 80 percent answer whenever practical. Resist the temptation to get trapped in "paralysis through analysis."

6. SYNTHESIZE YOUR FINDINGS

Step six is to synthesize your findings so you can communicate a digestible solution to the decision-maker. If you are the decision-maker, ensure that your team develops a coherent and concise message for communicating the recommendation. The key question from all of your research is, "What's the 'so what'?" In other words, what practical actions are implied by the findings so you can answer the question, "What should we *do* to solve the problem?"

I've often found this step to be the hardest. When faced with a basic problem like, "I need to know what time it is," many teams are inclined to respond by describing in detail how to build a watch. One technique that can help you synthesize your findings is a pyramid structure. Start with a foundation of common themes from the data and facts derived from your research. Then distill those upward into pillars of core logic supporting how to solve the problem. Finally, synthesize your core logic into a governing thought that clearly articulates your recommended solution.

7. PROPOSE YOUR SOLUTION

The final step is to propose your solution to the decision-maker by answering the question, "What should we do to solve the problem?" You've pulled the problem apart, analyzed the critical issues, and put the problem back together in a solvable way. Now it's time to present your recommendation. Focus on clarity and impact. Keep in mind that most decision-makers are busy, with a lot on their plates, so avoid the temptation to "build a watch" like we just discussed. Instead, get right to the point by starting with your governing thought at the top of your pyramid, and work down from there based on questions that arise from the decision-maker.

So far we've talked about operational changes that you may need to make as a leader in the face of uncertainty. Proactively, you can leverage the concept of *contingency planning* within the *Collaborative Planning Process* for changes that can be anticipated. For unanticipated problems, you can leverage the *Problem-Solving Process* that we just discussed to help you navigate unplanned operational changes. However, there will be other times when changes will need to occur at the strategic level, which can require innovation and organizational change. Some of the most common reasons driving the need for organizations to innovate and change include changes among customers, technology, the economy, politics, and your organizational dynamics.[103]

Leading Organizational Change

Change management guru John Kotter, a former leadership professor at Harvard Business School and author of the *New York Times* best-selling book *Leading Change*, says, "Perhaps the greatest challenge business leaders face today is how to stay competitive amid constant turbulence and disruption." Yet his research shows that most change efforts fail to achieve their intended result.[104] History is replete with examples of well-known companies that were once leaders in their respective industries, but failed to keep up with the speed of change. So how can you prevent your team from being left behind? More specifically, how do you effectively lead innovation and change within your organization?

Creating a Culture of Change

First, it's important to understand some of the primary inhibitors of innovation and organizational change. Comfort with the status quo, resource constraints, unmotivated employees, opposition from influential stakeholders, and competing interests or priorities are common drivers.[105]

Acknowledging these common inhibitors, next consider how to foster an innovative *culture* (remember the first dimension of our *leadership triad*). Ed Catmull, co-founder of Pixar and president of Walt Disney Animation Studios, asserts that successful innovation is less about personality, and more about process. It is rarely an "aha" moment. Usually innovation is the result of a painful, disciplined process underpinned by candid collaboration.[106] Peter Drucker, whom many have called "the founder of modern management," describes innovation as a purposeful search for new opportunities through the focused application of knowledge, hard work, and lessons learned from failure.[107]

In their book, *Collective Genius: The Art and Practice of Leading Innovation*, Linda Hill, Greg Brandeau, Emily Truelove, and Kent Lineback assert that "Innovation is a team sport" that almost always results from "multiple hands, not the genius of some solitary inventor." Moreover, they describe the essence of leading innovation as "setting the stage" so that others can perform on it.[108]

The *Collective Genius* authors also point out that innovation thrives in an environment characterized by diversity of thought, conflicting ideas, patience to test and learn from different approaches, and courage to integrate new possibilities. With this in mind, an effective leader can foster an innovative culture by creating a sense of community within their team where members are connected through a common purpose, shared values, and rules of engagement or behavioral guidelines.[109] Think back to the concept of your *leader's intent,* and consider how it might help you connect this type of culture to your mission in the context of a rapidly changing operating environment.

The bottom line is that implementing new ways of doing business requires transformational leadership. As you adjust and adapt your vision to keep up with a dynamic, rapidly-changing environment, you will need to assess your team's mission with a frequency that is correlated to the speed of change. Otherwise you will get stuck in the status quo, and your competitive advantage will begin to erode.

As you adjust your *mission*, you will need to connect your *people* to it by re-tuning how you articulate, reinforce, and illuminate the new mission. You'll also need to adjust your *leader's intent* to connect your *culture* to the new mission. And you may also need to emphasize an innovative mindset during *coaching and developing* sessions with your people, in order to help them embrace the culture of change.

Steps to Help Your Team Create and Sustain Organizational Change

Once you've established a culture that can embrace change, you can get down to the business of creating and sustaining change. In *Leading Change,* John Kotter describes some key reasons why change efforts fail, based on his research. They include complacency, lack of vision and guidance, obstacles, lack of momentum, and lack of follow-through.[110] Through my own personal experience with transformations in a number of organizations across a range of industries, I've learned seven important steps for creating and sustaining organizational change, which are highlighted below.

SEVEN STEPS TO CREATE AND SUSTAIN CHANGE

STEP	DESCRIPTION
1	Create a compelling case for change (a "burning platform" where people believe you must do something)
2	Initiate strategic communication from the top including the purpose and importance of the effort, and what success looks like (change vision)
3	Recruit key influencers to join your transformation team, and collaboratively develop a strategy to achieve the vision (generate buy-in)
4	Engage line-level stakeholders to create "champions" by helping them understand the importance of the effort and what's in it for them
5	Celebrate quick wins for momentum
6	Implement a high-visibility reporting cadence with top leadership
7	Embed results in organizational systems and culture for sustainability

1. CREATE A COMPELLING CASE FOR CHANGE
Identify a "burning platform" for your team so they can embrace the idea that you can't do nothing and must do *something*.

2. INITIATE STRATEGIC COMMUNICATION

It should come from top leadership, include the purpose and importance of the effort, and paint a picture of what success looks like. This is your *change vision*. Ensure it is clear and concise and that it cascades throughout the organization.

3. RECRUIT KEY INFLUENCERS

Actively pursue and persuade influential people within your organization to join your transformation team. Engage with them to help you collaboratively develop a strategy to achieve the vision. This will help generate top-down buy-in.

4. ENGAGE LINE-LEVEL STAKEHOLDERS

Identify key stakeholders on the front lines. Explain the importance of effort and what's in it for them. This will help generate grass-roots support by creating front-line champions.

5. CELEBRATE QUICK WINS

This will generate momentum by reinforcing your vision among key influencers, motivating front-line champions, and helping to get skeptics on board.

6. IMPLEMENT A HIGH-VISIBILITY REPORTING CADENCE

Progress should be measured and briefed to top leadership on a frequent basis. This will drive urgency and accountability into the effort and help get resisters on board.

7. EMBED RESULTS IN SYSTEMS AND CULTURE

This is the key to long-term sustainability. Changes can be codified in policy and processes. They can also be reflected in your leader's intent, where you connect your culture to your mission.

Most importantly, they should be role-modeled by leaders at all levels so that the change will stick.

Leading Through a Crisis

There is one final topic we need to cover about leading through uncertainty and change before we "land the plane" in this chapter. Regardless of how much you plan and how well you lead, you will inevitably encounter crises. I've encountered more than I'd like to remember. Nevertheless, I've learned some valuable lessons along the way about crisis leadership. Some of them I've learned the hard way. Others I've learned through more favorable outcomes. To help spare you the former and so that you can experience more of the latter, here are five things to think about the next time you find yourself leading your team through a crisis.

How to Help Your Team in a Crisis

1. RAPIDLY ANALYZE THE SITUATION

Huddle with your senior leadership team, including legal and public relations. Also bring into the conversation anyone who has a good grasp of the facts surrounding the crisis. Avoid the temptation to jump to conclusions or prematurely place blame. Focus on what happened, given what you currently know, what the implications and impacts are for people within and external to your organization, and what immediate actions you can take to help stem the crisis and mitigate further damage. Once aligned, initiate the immediate actions.

2. SHAPE YOUR COMMUNICATIONS

Focus on honesty and empathy. The key is to develop trust with people inside and outside your organization by taking responsibility, telling the truth, and acknowledging the emotional challenges people are experiencing as a result of the crisis. Develop a concise message that describes what happened, empathetically acknowledges the impact, and explains what you are doing about it. Do all of this quickly so you can drive the narrative, rather than react to it. Remember that bad news rarely, if ever, gets better with time.

3. EXERCISE VISIBLE LEADERSHIP

Step into the spotlight and be ready to take the heat for your team. This is far from comfortable, but it's one of the most important things you'll ever do as a leader. Remember our discussion about composure as it relates to your culture in chapter 1? This is your chance to let your true character shine in the face of real adversity. Start by sharing your message with your team and offer them the opportunity to ask questions. Instruct them to refer any media inquiries to your senior leadership team, because your next step is to deliver the same message to people outside your organization through a press release, press conference, video interview, social media, and/or other appropriate communication channels. Conclude by announcing that you've commenced an investigation (we'll talk about this in a second), and will update everyone as you learn more. Throughout this entire process, keep reminding yourself that accountability and transparency are your keys to developing trust.

4. CREATE A CRISIS ACTION TEAM

Carefully consider the expertise needed based on the nature of the crisis, and ensure the team has adequate information flow to create a data-driven, fact-based, common operating picture. Use the *Collaborative Planning Process* that we previously discussed in this chapter to rapidly generate potential courses of action. Begin by assessing the results of your immediate actions, and adjust next steps accordingly. Accelerate and iterate your COA decision cycle to stay ahead of the crisis, and make sure you have a plan to stay ahead of the media.

5. INITIATE AN INVESTIGATION

As soon as the crisis begins to stabilize, commence an investigation. Depending on the nature of the crisis, the investigation can be conducted formally or informally by an internal or external body. When deciding among these options, weigh the importance of resource intensity and speed versus the perception of objectivity and integrity. For example, an informal investigation conducted internally might be the fastest way to generate insights, but this may also increase the risk of cover-up allegations. On the other hand, a formal investigation by an external third party may be more thorough and objective, but this could also result in delayed insights, making it harder for you to stay ahead of the media. Consider balancing these risks by launching an informal, internal investigation to generate rapid initial insights, followed immediately by a formal, external investigation. Thoughtfully assess the expertise you need on the investigating team in order to ensure rigor and accuracy in the findings. Results of the investigation should address, at a minimum, two things: cause(s), and recommendations for how to prevent a similar crisis from occurring in the future. Use these findings to update your internal and external communications. Own your mistakes, vow to do better, and put into place measures for continuous improvement within your organization.

Although we've talked a lot about uncertainty in this chapter, one thing *is* certain. You will face crises as a leader. While we'd like to avoid them, they're unavoidable. I can't tell you when they will happen or what they will look like, but I can tell you that spears will fly and it won't be fun. It will feel lonely at the top, and you'll understand more deeply the burden of leadership. Perhaps you've been there. I know I have.

During times like these, I've found it helpful to remind myself of Theodore Roosevelt's words about "The Man in the Arena."[111]

> It is not the critic who counts; not the man who points out how the strong man stumbles, or where the doer of deeds could have done them better. The credit belongs to the man who is actually in the arena, whose face is marred by dust and sweat and blood; who strives valiantly; who errs, who comes short again and again, because there is no effort without error and shortcoming; but who does actually strive to do the deeds; who knows the great enthusiasms, the great devotions; who spends himself in a worthy cause; who at the best knows in the end the triumph of high achievement, and who at the worst, if he fails, at least fails while daring greatly, so that his place shall never be with those cold and timid souls who neither know victory nor defeat.

I encourage you to see crises as crucible opportunities that can help hone you as a leader and prepare you for greater things to come. If leadership was easy, anyone could do it. But leadership is hard. It's a marathon that requires intense determination and perseverance, especially during difficult times. There are plenty of people out there who can critique leaders during a crisis, but few who can actually lead with character, competence, and composure when the spears are flying.

Summary

I think Yogi Berra was spot-on when he said, "The future ain't what it used to be." The rate of change in the world today is accelerating more rapidly than ever. To be successful in this environment, high-performing leaders must expect uncertainty and embrace change in order to maintain a competitive advantage.

Collaborative planning and problem-solving with your team can help you navigate uncertainty and implement operational changes necessary to stay ahead of the curve. Transformational leadership can help you foster an innovative culture and create organizational changes required to adapt to a dynamic strategic landscape. And strong crisis leadership can help guide your team through the inevitable valleys along the way.

I find it interesting that after signing with the New York Yankees in 1943, Yogi Berra joined the U.S. Navy and served under General Eisenhower's command in the D-Day invasion at Normandy, where he manned a machine gun on a thirty-six-foot landing craft and later earned a Purple Heart. In a 2004 interview, television commentator Keith Olbermann asked Yogi, "What would happen to all of us if D-Day had failed? Have you ever thought about what our lives would have been like?" Yogi answered, "No, I never did think about it. I thought we had good generals there. Eisenhower was great."[112]

That's a pretty inspiring microcosm of leading through uncertainty, if you ask me. A nineteen-year-old in the midst of chaos and danger on the front lines of one of the largest, most complex military operations in history was confident in the outcome of the mission because he trusted his leader. And the leader was confident because he trusted his team to develop a good plan, and even more importantly, he trusted them to be able to rapidly adjust the plan to maintain an advantage because of their collaborative planning and preparation. You may not be certain of what's going to happen, but you can be certain that your people are prepared and working together if you've led them well. Something tells me that Yogi might have summed all of this up by saying, "Certainty is the best way to overcome uncertainty."

QUESTIONS FOR REFLECTION

- How can your team better manage volatility, uncertainty, complexity, and ambiguity?
- What can you do to become a better decision-maker?
- What does your team need to change to maintain a competitive advantage?

CHAPTER 9

LEVERAGING THE ESSENTIALS TO LEAD THROUGH INFLUENCE

"You don't need a title to be a leader."

—MARK SANBORN

During the culmination of academic commencement ceremonies every year, thousands of new graduates throw their caps in the air to celebrate their hard work and well-deserved accomplishments. The "hat toss" tradition originated at the U.S. Naval Academy in 1912. Graduating midshipmen who were becoming newly commissioned officers in the United States Navy and Marine Corps no longer needed their hats (called "covers" in military parlance), since they would be wearing officer covers from then on.

Over time, it became customary for visitors attending Annapolis graduations to retrieve one of the tossed covers as a keepsake following the ceremony. In 2018, one of those visitors was a young girl who was experiencing a series of intense personal challenges and highly emotional difficulties. She happened to pick up the cover tossed by James Winnefeld III, who had just been commissioned a second lieutenant in the U.S. Marine Corps.

Inside the cover she found a note that read:

> To Whomever Grabbed My Cover,
>
> If you are reading this, it is likely that you know someone commissioning with the great Class of 2018. It is also likely that, like many of us graduating today, you have some pretty lofty goals, dreams, or aspirations. So, I wanted to write you a letter about one of the fundamental principles for achieving your goals: overcoming adversity.
>
> Over the course of my time at the Academy, I have found myself faced with adversity on numerous occasions. Each time I was given a series of choices. Do I take the easy way or the hard way? Will I be defined by the situation or will I define the situation? Will I let my emotions get the better of me, or will I control them?
>
> What I learned from this adversity is that the only thing we can control is our emotions and how we react to what life hands us. How you act in your times of adversity defines your character. No one else can do this for you. How you react to adversity is a conscious decision only you can make. Take control of your emotions, take control of your actions. Turn negatives into positives. Life will find a way to hit you hard. When this happens, get back up, keep moving, and become better because of it.
>
> Semper Fi.

In tears, the young girl approached her mom and asked her to have the letter framed so she could hang it on her bedroom wall. Then her mom, after noticing a cell phone number on the cover's nametag, sent Second Lieutenant Winnefeld an emotional text, thanking him for the profound impact he had on her daughter.[113]

Second Lieutenant Winnefeld knew a thing or two about leadership. His father was Admiral James Winnefeld Jr., who had recently retired as the Vice Chairman of the Joint Chiefs of Staff. His grandfather was Rear Admiral James Winnefeld Sr., Annapolis Class of 1951. But he also knew a lot about influence, in the way that he helped shape that young girl's outlook on life.

You don't have to be in an official position of authority with direct reports to be a leader. You can be a leader just by making people around you better. This can happen with people who work closely with you but don't report to you. Or it can happen with people who don't work with you every day but are influenced by your actions and words. It can even happen with people you've never met, like the girl who found James Winnefeld's cover.

The topic of leading through influence is becoming increasingly important, because more and more organizations are becoming flatter and less hierarchical. Cross-functional teams are more common as organizations aspire to be more "agile" in today's rapidly changing environment. Teams are experiencing an increased reliance on external contractors and subcontractors. And organizational growth requires more cross-functional collaboration in order to achieve and sustain high performance. In each of these cases, you may not have formal positional authority, but you're still responsible for getting things done. That's why this final chapter is about leading through influence.

The key question in this chapter is, "How do you influence a diverse group of people to work together toward a common goal when you don't necessarily have positional authority?"

Let's start by answering the question, "What is influence?"

I define influence as the ability to shape others' perspectives, feelings, beliefs, goals, and/or actions. I've also found that influence in the context of leadership is closely tied to persuasion, which I would describe as the ability to effectively change mindsets and behaviors. When you don't have positional authority, persuasion is an extremely important skill that can help you influence people with diverse perspectives to work together toward a goal.

But even if you *do* have positional authority, I've learned that influence and persuasion are also important for effective leadership. Why? Because relying on authoritative control is not an effective way to lead, at least not in today's world.

Authoritative control may have been an effective leadership approach during industrial-age decades past, but in my experience it doesn't work very well in today's information-age environment. The information revolution has democratized data and decentralized information to the point where nearly everyone can have an informed opinion and a voice. "Because I told you so" is just not effective anymore. It may work temporarily in the short term for some organizations, but overall I've found it doesn't lead to sustained high performance in the long run. In today's military or any other high-performing team where the goal is to empower people to think critically and creatively, collaboration and persuasion are particularly important.

In order to provide a foundation for leading through influence, let's consider both the *art* (philosophical foundation) and *science* (psychological foundation) of influence.

The Art (Philosophy) of Influence

First, the *art* of influence can be traced to the fourth century BC, when the Greek philosopher Aristotle developed his "equation of persuasion" which included three elements:[114]

- *Logos* (the Greek word for *reason*, from which we get the word *logic*)
- *Pathos* (the Greek word for *emotions* or *feelings*, from which we get the word *passion*)
- *Ethos* (the Greek word for *character* in relation to the credibility of the presenter, from which we get the word *ethics*)

For someone to have the best likelihood of persuading an individual or a group of people, Aristotle argued that these three elements should be leveraged in unison. In other words, effective influencers speak from a position of character and credibility, and they appeal to others through a combination of reason and emotion in order to shape their perspectives, feelings, beliefs, goals, and/or actions.

In many ways, the art of influence is even more important today than it was in Aristotle's world, over 2,000 years ago. As our world has transitioned from the industrial age to the information age, we have also moved from a manufacturing-based economy to one that is knowledge-driven. "Ideas are the currency of the twenty-first century. The ability to persuade, to change hearts and minds, is perhaps the single greatest skill that will give you a competitive edge in the knowledge economy—an age where ideas matter more than ever," says Harvard University instructor and *Wall Street Journal* best-selling author Carmine Gallo, president of Gallo Communications Group.[115]

So how can you apply Aristotle's principles to persuade others on your team to work together, turning ideas into action toward a common goal? Start with the *leadership triad*. The three key leadership qualities for creating a high-performing *culture*—your character, competence, and composure—provide the foundation for your ethos and credibility. Creating a sense of purpose for your team in the form of your *mission* provides the reason (logos) why your team exists. And inspiring your *people* with a sense of value and meaning (pathos) is the key to connecting them passionately to your mission.

With this foundation, next think about ways to leverage credibility, reason, and emotion on a personal level in your day-to-day interactions. Regarding credibility, focus on personal relationships and connections with your teammates that establish trust. Remember from chapter 1 that trust is the center of gravity of a high-performing culture. With respect to reason, do your homework and develop logical arguments by analyzing data and assembling facts in a way that creates actionable information. Finally, think of ways to engender emotions that can move your teammates to action.

One of the best ways to inspire emotions in others is through storytelling. Recent studies have found that hearing stories triggers the release of oxytocin in our brain.[116] Recall from our discussion in chapter 6 about providing effective feedback, that oxytocin heightens our ability to trust others and enhances emotional agreement.

In the 500 most popular TED Talks of all time, on average 65 percent of each speaker's time was comprised of stories, 25 percent of their time involved analysis, and 10 percent was devoted to establishing the credibility of the speaker. Lesson learned: the most popular influencers wrap their ideas into a story.[117]

What kinds of stories should you use? Ones that create a personal connection. They don't have to be long. They just need to be stories or anecdotes that are meaningful to you, relevant to the situation, and told in an authentic way. Although they require the most vulnerability, examples of adversity, failure, and lessons learned the hard way are often the most effective at developing personal connections that can move people to action.[118]

The Science (Psychology) of Influence

The emotional element of persuasion that we just discussed is a good segue to the *science* of influence, or the psychological foundations of persuasion which are rooted in behavioral science and behavioral economics (where we get the term "buy-in"). Robert Cialdini, author of the *New York Times* best-selling book *Influence: The Psychology of Persuasion*, says, "Persuasion skills exert far greater influence over others' behavior than formal power structures do." Based on his research, Cialdini lists six principles of effective persuasion:[119]

- Liking—people tend to like those who like them
- Reciprocity—people tend to repay in kind
- Social proof—people tend to follow popular opinions
- Consistency—people tend to align with clear commitments from others
- Authority—people tend to defer to experts
- Scarcity—people tend to want more of what they can have less of

Maybe you have experience with some or perhaps all of these principles. Have you ever been inclined to agree with someone during a meeting because they're always respectful and friendly?

When someone has gone out of their way to help you with something in the past, have you felt more willing to support their position during a discussion? During a group debate, have you ever felt the momentum shift one way or the other with the tide of group consensus? When someone clearly and publicly commits to something, do you find it easier for you to get behind it? Has there ever been a time when you were stuck on a tough problem with your team, and a member with an abundance of experience and deep expertise weighed in with a recommendation that unlocked the path forward? And have you ever felt or benefitted from the "fear of missing out" (FOMO), especially if you are in the business of sales and marketing or raising capital investments? If your answer to any of these questions is "yes" then you've experienced the psychology of persuasion.

Diving deeper into the science of influence, it's also important to further understand neurochemical factors affecting the brain. The three main parts of the human brain are the neocortex, which is used primarily for data processing (logic and reason); the limbic system, which controls emotions; and the brain stem and other structures, which are primarily concerned with safety and threat avoidance.[120]

What's important to realize is that the human brain is addicted to being right and avoids threats of being wrong. When you are "winning" an argument, your brain is flooded with the addictive hormones adrenaline and dopamine, which reward you with a feeling of dominance. Under threat or stress, however, cortisol floods the brain—shutting down advanced thought processes like strategy, compassion, and trust. This causes us to enter protection mode from the shame or loss of status associated with being wrong (remember in chapter 3 the point about "deflector shields" coming down when people start pointing fingers during a debrief?). And this generally leads to one of four responses:[121]

- Fight (argue louder)
- Flight (hide behind group consensus)
- Freeze (disengage and be quiet)
- Appease (agree)

For the purpose of self-awareness, do you find yourself gravitating toward one of these responses more often than not when you feel psychologically threatened? If so, can you recognize it the next time it happens and find a way to maintain your conviction and composure under stress? For example, I'll never forget the time I was coaching a senior leadership team a few weeks after discussing these neurochemical factors with them in a separate forum. At one point during the coaching session, one of the executives made a comment that indirectly threatened another team member's competence. As the tension in the room mounted and everyone looked at the other team member to see how he would react, he smiled and responded, "Give me a minute. Cortisol is flooding my brain right now." We all started laughing and the tension immediately dissolved.

> Effective influence is highly dependent upon psychological safety.

So how do these psychological fundamentals apply to leading through influence? The bottom line is, effective influence is highly dependent upon psychological safety.[122] Recall from our discussion in chapter 6 about coaching and developing your team, that a psychologically safe culture is a requirement for resolving conflict in a healthy way. Extrapolating this a bit further, you could argue that the essence of influencing others is resolving conflicts among differing perspectives, feelings, beliefs, goals, and/or actions.

Furthermore, a 2012 study by Google revealed that an environment of psychological safety is the most important characteristic of a high-performing team. The study was called *Project Aristotle.* It was the sequel to *Project Oxygen* which, as you also recall from chapter 6, studied the characteristics of a great manager. *Project Aristotle* examined the characteristics of effective teams and concluded that the top trait of a highly-effective team is an atmosphere where team members "feel confident that no one on the team will embarrass or punish anyone else for admitting a mistake, asking a question, or offering a new idea."[123]

To foster an environment of psychological safety, consider five principles:

- Actively seek others' opinions
- Put yourself in their shoes and try to genuinely understand where they are coming from
- Respect the value of their perspectives
- Keep an open mind
- Demonstrate willingness to be persuaded and influenced yourself

You can also consider using context and contrast to help move people in a nonthreatening way from a current mindset to a new one. Context, or explaining the big picture, can help create the case for change. Contrast, or comparing the status quo to the realm of the possible, can help confirm the case for change. An effective technique for creating contrast is to use before and after stories from similar experiences. Another is to use visual tools such as graphics, images, or pictures that can help simplify complex ideas to help people imagine moving from the current situation to a better one.[124]

Applications of Influence

You might be asking, "But how can I apply all of these concepts about persuasion and influence in an authentic way without appearing as though I'm trying to manipulate people?"

It's a good question.

I've found that there are two keys to leading through influence in an authentic way. First, demonstrate genuine humility, teachability, and influenceability yourself. Second, focus on generating the best team solution for the broader good, rather than pursuing personal agendas. If you consistently do these two things, I've found that people will generally trust your intentions.

How to Influence "Up"

You might also be asking, "What about influencing 'up'? How can I influence my boss and other more senior leaders?" That's another good question. I've found that there are four things that can help. First, focus on how your objectives fit into your overall organizational goals. Second, conduct a thorough cost-benefit analysis. As you've probably experienced, it's hard to argue with someone who can clearly describe how their efforts are supporting the larger organization's mission and explain how the potential benefits outweigh the costs.

A third technique that can help you influence "up" is one I learned the hard way and wish I'd learned much earlier in my professional career. As a junior military officer, I felt like I needed to have all of the answers about a situation or problem before briefing my boss on a recommended solution. Not having the answer to a question they might ask could indicate gaps in thoroughness or competence on my part.

Looking back, I can see this mindset was a valuable part of our culture, because it forced me to take responsibility and think through problems rigorously before recommending solutions. But now I realize it also caused me to miss valuable opportunities to incorporate my boss's experience early in my thinking, which could have helped me solve problems more efficiently and effectively.

As I was promoted into more senior positions where I was sitting on the "other side of the table" with junior officers briefing me on situations and problems, I gained an appreciation for how rewarding it is for leaders to have the opportunity to mentor their people and provide perspectives from their own experiences that can be valuable in helping to shape solutions. I also learned how important it is to keep your boss informed about certain situations while they are still evolving in order to enhance situational awareness and trust . . . especially considering the speed at which information travels.

One Friday morning halfway through my final assignment as a Marine aircraft group commander, I was in one of our squadron's briefing rooms with seven other FA-18 pilots and weapons systems officers preparing for a local training flight. We were scheduled to land around noon, which would allow me time to debrief and make it to the change of command ceremony for the air station commander later that afternoon.

Just before finishing our brief, the squadron duty officer opened the door with a nervous look on his face and informed us that we needed to evacuate the building immediately due to a potential truck bomb parked next to the hangar. Leaving everything behind, my BlackBerry phone included, we quickly evacuated and reassembled in a location safely away from the building.

While military police and detectives who had just arrived on scene were describing to me what they knew, the squadron commander approached me and asked to have a word. He calmly explained that he had good reasons to believe that the barrels of fuel that someone had spotted in the back of the enclosed truck were just that—barrels of fuel that were in the process of being moved from one location to another. He was a seasoned commander, and I had a great deal of trust in his judgment. He recommended that we should obviously keep the area cordoned off while we continued to investigate, but that we should avoid overreacting. As we discussed potential courses of action together, I trusted his judgment even more.

An hour later, our explosive ordinance team verified what the squadron commander originally told me. In the meantime, my boss's boss (three-star general) had landed at the air station for the change of command ceremony that afternoon. He was told there was a "truck bomb situation" unfolding, and immediately called my boss. Then my boss called me. Of course, my Black-Berry was still inside the briefing room. Which explained why my executive officer was suddenly sprinting toward me waving his BlackBerry and screaming, "Sir, you need to call the wing commanding general NOW!"

Remarkably composed considering the circumstances, my boss asked, "What's going on, and why am I hearing about this from my boss?" After twenty-four years in the Marine Corps, you'd think I'd have learned by now how to do a better job of keeping my boss informed while I solved evolving problems. What I should have done is make a quick call to say: "Boss, here's the situation. I don't have all the facts yet, but here's what I do know and what I'm doing about it. I'll keep you updated as the situation unfolds, but I wanted to make sure you have situational awareness and see if you have any additional guidance or advice." That conversation would have gone a long way to keep my boss informed and enhance trust, much in the same way that the squadron commander enhanced my trust by problem-solving with me while the situation was still developing.

In the course of my leadership coaching in the private sector, I've shared this story with a number of junior and senior leaders alike. Many of the junior leaders can relate with the expectation to have all of the answers before they present a recommended solution to their boss. Many of the senior leaders wish junior leaders would loop them in earlier, because it keeps them informed and provides a valuable mentoring opportunity that can help shape the solution and enhance trust.

Lesson learned: don't hesitate to ask your boss to problem-solve together with you early in the solution-development process. An effective way to approach this is to do your initial homework (time permitting, of course), and then start the conversation with, "Boss, here's the situation, and here's what I'm thinking. I'd love to hear if you have any additional thoughts or perspectives." I think you'll find they will enjoy the chance to share their experience, appreciate the opportunity to help shape the solution, and trust you more for valuing their perspectives. And whatever you do, if the situation is dynamically evolving and time-critical, don't do what I did.

The fourth technique I've found effective for influencing "up," especially if your boss is exceptionally busy or less inclined to problem-solve with you, is to seize the initiative. You've probably heard the saying, "It's better to beg for forgiveness than to ask for permission." The only problem is, I've seen that backfire more than once. I think a better approach is to operate with an "unless directed otherwise" mindset.

This means when you are faced with a situation requiring action (or even better, when you see one developing on the horizon), use the techniques we discussed in the previous chapter to figure out what you believe is the best thing to do about it. Then send a note to your boss briefly describing the situation, followed by, "Unless directed otherwise, I intend to . . ." I think you'll find they will appreciate and respect your initiative.

Of course, they always have the option to ask, "Have you thought about . . . ?" or say, "I'd like to learn more about this, so let's find time to discuss." More often, you're likely to get a green light in the form of, "Sounds good, please keep me updated." Perhaps even more common is no response, which can be interpreted as "silence is consent" as long as you are sure they received the message.

> You've probably heard the saying, "It's better to beg for forgiveness than to ask for permission." The only problem is, I've seen that backfire more than once. I think a better approach is to operate with an "unless directed otherwise" mindset.

Bottom line, your boss and other senior leaders have a lot of issues on their plate. If you can seize the initiative and stay ahead of them on *your* issues, you have a reasonable chance of being able to influence their perspectives. And in the process, you are likely to earn their appreciation for your initiative and their respect for your judgment as a leader.

What If Your Boss Is Difficult?

These four techniques for influencing "up" assume that your boss is relatively reasonable and persuadable. But what if they're not? What if they are arrogant, stubborn, narcissistic, and disagreeable? If this describes your boss, I feel your pain. If it's any consolation, you're not alone. That's how Steve Jobs was described by his team at Apple early in his career, according to Wharton Business School organizational psychologist Adam Grant, who has spent a lot of time with Apple team members who were somehow able to influence the visionary genius to occasionally change his views.[125]

For many years, Steve Jobs was adamant that he would never produce a smartphone. He thought they were for "geeks with pocket protectors." But in 2005, his team eventually persuaded him to change his mind. Within a decade, the iPhone had generated over one trillion dollars in revenue. And today, Apple is the most valuable company in the world.[126]

How did they do it? By asking questions instead of asserting their opinions. In previous chapters we've talked a lot about how asking questions can help you as a leader. In chapter 5 we discussed how questions can help you inspire and empower your team. In chapter 6 we explored how questions can help you coach and develop your team. Questions can also be an effective way to help you influence your boss or other senior leaders in your organization, especially if they are "difficult."

It goes without saying that arrogant, stubborn, narcissistic, disagreeable people tend to react defensively when challenged directly, often due to underlying insecurity. Perhaps you've learned this the hard way. A more effective way to influence a boss who exhibits one or more of these qualities, is to ask questions that spark them to rethink their own views.[127]

For example, rather than highlight an arrogant leader's lack of knowledge about an issue, instead ask them to explain how a certain part of the issue works, in order to help them see gaps in their understanding. If your boss is stubborn, ask questions like, "What if . . . ?" or "How could we . . . ?" that allow them to take control of the solution. If you want to change the mind of a narcissist, compliment them on a strength unrelated to the issue you want to discuss, and then address the issue in the form of a question. And if your boss tends to be disagreeable, ask questions that tap into their competitive energy.[128]

One of the key questions that ultimately changed Steve Jobs's mind about the iPhone tapped into his competitive zeal toward rival Microsoft. His team asked the question, "Won't there eventually be a Windows phone?" And the rest is history.[129]

The Influence Pyramid

A PRACTICAL FRAMEWORK FOR
LEADING THROUGH INFLUENCE

DEPENDABILITY — Follow through: be reliable, responsive, and results-oriented

EXPERTISE — Demonstrate the value of your knowledge, experience, and network

RESPECT — Be inclusive, use "we" instead of "I," value others' opinions, be influenceable yourself

CONTEXT — Talk about the big picture and the broader good, generate alignment through vision

CONNECTION — Start by building relationships, identify shared interests, find common ground

Tying together all of these concepts about the philosophy and psychology of persuasion, I've found the simple framework above helpful to me when thinking about how to practically apply the art and science of leading through influence.

In my experience, relationships are the foundation of influence. Thus, I believe leading through influence starts with *connection*. Focus on identifying shared interests and objectives, and finding common ground to develop trust.

Next, establish *context*. Talk about the big picture and the broader good, and generate alignment through vision to help people see what is possible.

Third, show *respect*. Be inclusive. Use "we" instead of "I" (remember there is no "I" in "team"). Genuinely value others' opinions, and be influenceable yourself.

Fourth, contribute your *expertise*. Demonstrate the value of your knowledge, experience, and network.

Finally, demonstrate *dependability*. Follow through by being reliable, responsive, and results-oriented.

Have you ever worked with someone who was especially skilled at building connections, establishing context, showing respect, contributing expertise, and demonstrating dependability? I've had the privilege of working with several, and they were always some of the most influential people in the organization, irrespective of their official position or number of direct reports. They tend to generate their own "company credibility" with a wide range of informal but loyal followers.

> Leading through influence starts with connection.

I believe the daily, practical application of the *influence pyramid* is important enough that it's worth memorizing, so I remember it using the acrostic "C-CRED" which is a shortened spin-off from "company credibility." It helps me stay focused on connections, context, respect, expertise, and dependability. It also reminds me that anyone and everyone can lead through influence, because people who do these five things well generate *trust* among their colleagues and team members. And as we've mentioned often in the previous chapters, trust is the center of gravity of effective leadership.

Generating Alignment

Sometimes people are assigned a leadership role where they are forced to lead through influence because they don't have formal positional authority. A common example of this is a cross-functional team that is formed to tackle a short-term project. One question that often comes up when discussing this type of situation is, "How do you generate consensus?" My answer usually is, "You don't need to." And then most ask, "Well, then how do you make decisions and get anything done?" And I'll respond, "Focus on alignment instead." Which typically leads to the question, "What's the difference?"

It's a great question. I like to think about alignment as a mutual commitment toward a common goal, even though people might be approaching the goal from different perspectives. Let's unpack three important implications from this definition.

First, there may be *different perspectives* within the team. In fact, I'd argue that there intentionally *should* be different perspectives among the team, because diversity of thought leads to productive debate, which creates a sharper solution. As we've

> Alignment is a mutual commitment toward a common goal, even though people might be approaching the goal from different perspectives.

previously discussed, this requires a psychologically safe atmosphere to be effective.

Second, there needs to be a *common goal*. Sometimes the goal is directed from higher authority. Other times it's developed internally within the team. In the latter case, the team leader needs to influentially leverage context and purpose to create a vision that everyone can aim toward, even though they may have different perspectives on how to get there.

Third, the leader needs to facilitate an open discussion that generates *mutual commitment* from all of the team members toward the common goal. This means ensuring that everyone's perspective is both heard and valued, while skillfully influencing the various viewpoints toward the common goal. At the same time, team members must keep an open mind and recognize that the leader is ultimately accountable for the team's progress and results.

Eventually a decision will need to be made. At this point, an aligned team—knowing that everyone's perspective was heard, valued, and included—will support the leader's decision, even though they may not completely agree. The diagram below helps me visualize the difference between *alignment* and *consensus*.[130]

ALIGNMENT VERSUS CONSENSUS

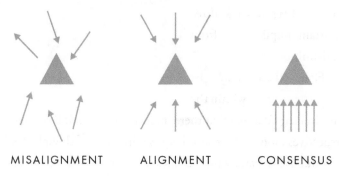

MISALIGNMENT   ALIGNMENT   CONSENSUS

The arrows in each picture within the diagram represent the perspective of each member on the team. The triangle represents the goal.

On the left, each team member contributes a different perspective, but they are not aligned toward the same goal. The resulting misalignment is likely to stagnate the team's progress and stifle results.

On the right, all of the members share nearly the same perspective and are aligned toward the same goal. Although this may produce a relatively fast and easy decision, the consensus can heighten groupthink and increase the risk of blind spots that may reduce decision quality.

In the center, each team member contributes a different perspective, and they are all aligned toward the common goal. Although they may not all agree on how to achieve the goal, they are mutually committed to it nonetheless. Their diverse perspectives provide the foundation for productive debate, which ultimately sharpens the quality of the decision. And once the decision is made, they all agree to support it.

Generating alignment through influence is definitely not easy. However, there are three techniques that you might find helpful if you are assigned a leadership position without formal organizational authority: apply the influence pyramid, decouple ideas from the people who thought of them, and explain to your team how much you value each member's input.

The first technique is to apply the *influence pyramid* that we just discussed in this chapter (remember "C-CRED"). Hopefully you'll have a head start through *connections* you've already begun to build with your colleagues on a personal level. *Context* can help you create a vision and crystallize the common goal for your team. *Respect* for your teammates will engender their mutual respect and create a psychologically safe environment for healthy discussion and debate. Drawing on your team members' *expertise* will enrich the debate and help sharpen the solution, as your own expertise adds credibility to your role. Finally, your *dependability* will generate trust, which as we've previously discussed is the center of gravity of effective leadership.

The second technique applies to the discussion and debate phase of team alignment. Specifically, it involves decoupling ideas from the people who thought of them in order to help mitigate natural bias toward one's own perspectives. The first step is to brainstorm together as a team with the caveat that there is no such thing as a dumb or crazy idea. You may need to draw ideas out of some of your less vocal team members, and you might need to regulate others who tend to be exceedingly vocal. Ensure everyone knows that their voice is important, and capture all of the ideas on a whiteboard or in a document that the entire team can see. Then once the brain dump is complete, ask everyone to take the "who" out of it and forget about which ideas are theirs. At this point, shift the focus to assessing all of the ideas objectively as a group. And if you happen to have a team member who is still fixated on their own idea, I've found it useful to ask them to play devil's advocate to help expand the team's thinking.

> Even if people disagree with our decision, they can align with it if they feel valued, respected, and appreciated throughout the process.

But even if you are the world's most influential leader and you've masterfully applied the first two techniques, invariably there will be at least one member of your team who may not be fully on board with the direction you are leaning. This is where the third technique might be helpful. Genuinely express to your team how much you value their input. Explain that their diversity of perspectives is what enabled you to arrive at what you believe is the sharpest solution and best decision for the team given the timeline you're operating under. Describe *why* you chose this particular solution for your decision. Then humbly acknowledge that you know some of them don't agree, but that you would appreciate their support. In the end, I've found that even if people disagree with our decision, they can align with it if they feel valued, respected, and appreciated throughout the process.

Summary

I would be remiss if I didn't close the loop here and explain the connection between leading through influence and the *leadership triad*. Recall that the key to leading through influence when you don't have positional authority is your ability to create alignment. We defined alignment as a mutual commitment toward a common goal, even though people might be approaching the goal from different perspectives.

Then we drew three important implications from that definition. First, diversity of thought that's enabled in a psychologically safe environment is a force multiplier for your team. Second, there needs to be a common goal. And third, respecting and valuing every team member's

> The environment that enables diversity of thought to thrive is your culture. The common goal is your mission. Respecting and valuing your people are how you inspire and align them toward your goal.

perspective is vital for discovering the best solution and creating alignment toward your goal.

Can you see the connections? The environment that enables diversity of thought to thrive is your *culture*. The common goal is your *mission*. Respecting and valuing your *people* are how you inspire and align them toward your goal. In other words, we've just come full circle back to the *leadership triad*, which is the foundation for leading through influence.

Our key question at the beginning of this chapter was, "How do you influence a diverse group of people to work together toward a common goal, when you don't necessarily have positional authority?" I hope I've helped you answer that question. For many years, serving in both the military and the private sector, my personal definition of leadership has been, "The art of influencing a diverse group of

> Leadership is the art of influencing a diverse group of people to work together toward a common goal.

people to work together toward a common goal." As you can see, I believe influence is inherently central to effective leadership, with or without positional authority. So it's only fitting that I finish by attempting to persuade you to consider one final thought. Even if you are in a position of authority, you can often be a more effective leader by leading through influence first, and relying on your authority as a last resort.

QUESTIONS FOR REFLECTION

- Where can you apply the art and science of persuasion to be a more influential leader?
- How can you do a better job of influencing your boss?
- Where can you use influence to more effectively generate alignment?

CONCLUSION

I was walking to dinner one evening with my good friend Adrian Gottschalk, who is the CEO of Foghorn Therapeutics, a biotechnology company in Cambridge, Massachusetts. We were discussing how easy it is for some people to take for granted how hard it is to be a good leader. I was struck by a comment that he made, comparing leadership to entropy. It had been more than thirty years since I seriously considered that word in a college thermodynamics class, but I vaguely remembered something about a natural tendency for the energy within a system to dissipate over time, resulting in a constant state of disorder and decline.

He continued his analogy by explaining that the amount of energy leaders need to continuously put into their organization to create and sustain a high-performing team is exponentially higher than the energy required to lead an average team. Moreover, bad leaders tend to suck the energy out of their team, which accelerates decline. I looked up "entropy" later that evening and learned that the Greek root word means "change within." I think Adrian hit the nail on the head regarding why leadership is so hard. Creating positive change within your team requires tremendous energy and focus.

As I mentioned in the introduction, my goal in writing this book is to make leadership less difficult for you. I know you are extremely busy and have a lot on your plate. It's hard to maintain work-life balance. You're under pressure. Your problems seem to never end. Some of them feel insurmountable. Your mission is challenging and targets are constantly changing. The adversity you are facing feels overwhelming at times. People are complex, and your bandwidth is limited. The burden of leadership is heavy. I understand.

I want to encourage and challenge you to focus your time and energy on your culture, people, and mission. Work on keeping those three areas connected through your leader's intent, inspiring and empowering your team, and coaching and developing your people. And try to keep your focus balanced, embrace uncertainty as an opportunity for change, and lead more through influence.

I know it won't be easy. Although the framework we've built and unpacked together in the previous nine chapters might seem relatively simple in theory, it's quite difficult in practice. Because at the top of the *leadership triad*, it takes personal accountability to focus on your culture. At the bottom left, it requires self-sacrifice to focus on your people. And at the bottom right, it takes self-discipline to focus on your mission. It's hard but worth it, because the difference you can make in helping your people and your team reach their full potential is amazing. And in the process, you will reach your full potential as a leader.

In closing, I'd like to introduce you to one of my personal heroes who was a rookie fighter pilot on an aircraft carrier exactly fifty years before I was—but under far more demanding conditions than anything I ever encountered or can even imagine.

"Butch" O'Hare grew up in the Midwest. He entered the U.S. Naval Academy in 1933, and graduated in 1937. He became a Naval Aviator when the United States was on the brink of

World War II, learned to fly the F4F Wildcat, and was assigned to the aircraft carrier USS *Lexington*.

In February 1942, American forces in the South Pacific were preparing the way for a two-pronged island-hopping campaign toward the Philippines and Japan. The USS *Lexington* was assigned the mission of penetrating the eastern perimeter of Japanese-controlled waters near the Solomon Islands.

On February 20, 1942, the *Lexington* came under attack by two waves of Japanese bombers. As the second wave approached, Lieutenant O'Hare and his wingman in their F4Fs were the only available fighters remaining on the flight deck. So Butch and his wingman launched. But when they joined up, they discovered that the wingman's gun was jammed.

As the last line of defense, outnumbered nine-to-one, Butch O'Hare attacked the enemy formation in the face of intense machine gun fire. He shot down five of the Japanese bombers and damaged a sixth. When he ran out of ammunition, he turned away the remaining three bombers through a series of intentional near-mid-air collisions.

As a result, he saved the USS *Lexington*, became the U.S. Navy's first "ace" (pilot who shot down five or more enemy aircraft) during World War II, and was the first Naval Aviator ever to receive the Congressional Medal of Honor. Today, Chicago's O'Hare International Airport is named after him. The next time you're there, make sure you check out the memorial that stands in his honor, between Terminals 1 and 2.

Rewind the clock twenty years earlier to the 1920s, when Al Capone practically owned Chicago through organized crime.

Capone had a lawyer named Easy Eddie who was exceptionally skilled at keeping him out of jail. As a result, Capone paid Eddie extremely well and bought him a huge mansion with bodyguards and live-in help. Eddie even had a son for whom he was able to provide everything that money could buy.

But in 1930, Eddie decided to turn in Capone. Some believe that one of his reasons was to provide something for his son that money couldn't buy—an example of character and integrity that his son could be proud of.

So Eddie testified against Capone, who was convicted and sent to prison. Eight years later when Capone was released, it cost Eddie his life when he was gunned down in a blaze of machine gun fire on a secluded Chicago street. The year was 1939—the same year that Eddie's son, Butch O'Hare, was in flight training preparing for World War II.[131]

I tell this story for two reasons. First, because we all make mistakes. All of us have failed as a leader at one time or another. Many of us have failed many times. Some of us have trouble putting the past behind us. Others of us feel like it's too late to make a difference. But it is never too late to do the right thing, to take care of the people entrusted to our leadership, and to focus on doing what's important.

> It is never too late to do the right thing, to take care of the people entrusted to our leadership, and to focus on doing what's important.

The second reason I tell the story is because our impact as a leader is often hard to measure. It's easy to get discouraged. We wonder if we are making a difference. Leadership is difficult and sometimes lonely. But I can guarantee you one thing. People are watching you—more closely than you know. And your opportunity to make a difference in their lives and have a positive impact on the world is greater than you can imagine.

This is why it has been such a privilege to have the opportunity to share with you what I've learned about the substance of leadership through my own journey. Thank you for investing your valuable time to come along for the ride. My hope is that some of the things I've shared will help you become a better leader. And in the process, that those you lead will feel more inspired, more empowered, and more fulfilled in your team's journey toward reaching your full potential.

ACKNOWLEDGMENTS

I've done a lot of difficult things in my life. Writing my first book is near the top of the list. The blank page at the beginning seemed like such a daunting mountain to climb. I'm not usually a procrastinator, but I became one in this case.

As I look back, I think there are a number of reasons why. At first, I had no idea how I was going to fill up an entire book. Then I soon realized I had the opposite problem: how to synthesize and organize everything that I believe matters most about leadership into a book people would actually read. At that point, self-doubt kicked in as I wondered, *Is anyone actually going to read this?*

This self-doubt compounded my perfectionist tendencies, making the process even harder. I also knew I needed to write conversationally, which isn't natural for me, given that most of my prior writing experiences were academic requirements. There were times when I was sure I could see my professor's red ink circling words on my computer screen while I typed.

Perhaps hardest of all, though, was overcoming the fear of throwing my personal experiences, emotions, and thoughts about leadership out there for the whole world to consume and critique. But my mind kept coming back to one thought: *If this book helps one leader out there to lead better, then it's all worth it.* If you're reading this far, I hope that leader is you.

I wouldn't have started this journey, and I certainly wouldn't have finished it, if not for the influence, help, and support of a number of people to whom I am extremely indebted and especially grateful.

First and foremost, I give thanks to God for the opportunities I've had to lead, learn, and serve. I am particularly thankful for His strength, wisdom, and guidance through every step of my leadership journey. As a follower of Christ, I'm grateful for His leadership example of humility, service, and sacrifice. Most of all, I am immeasurably grateful for the gift of eternal life through His sacrificial love and amazing grace, despite my flaws and failures.

To my dad and mom, Robbie and Joyce Robinson, thank you for the foundation of faith and moral values you instilled in me growing up, which shaped me as a person and leader. Your actions always spoke louder than your words when teaching me the importance of character, integrity, and treating people like you would want to be treated. I'm not sure where I'd be without your love, wisdom, and guidance over the years. I've been blessed with the best parents a son could ask for, and I love and appreciate you both more than words can adequately express.

To my younger brother, Dan, thank you for your leadership example. I look up to you more than you know. I admire the impact and influence you've had on so many people during your Marine Corps aviation career. I'm also proud to agree with those in our common professional sphere who know both Colonel Robinsons and ask me, "How did your brother get all the brains in the family?" Thank you for always being there for me as a thought partner throughout the years, and for your unwavering support and mentorship during many of my leadership challenges along the way.

To my youngest brother, Rob, thank you for inspiring me to persevere, especially during the tough times. Although your health challenges have been disabling and debilitating, your mind and spirit are brighter than ever. Thank you for being there with me at the beginning of my transition from the military to the private sector, helping me imagine what the next chapter in my leadership journey could look like, and for all of your support since then. And thank you for being there again to help edit my first draft of this book. In addition to your superb editing advice, I'll never forget your first reaction: "Dave, as a former sociology professor, I've read a lot of dense material in my life, but there are a couple of chapters in there that might top them all." Among your many excellent recommendations, thank you for helping me decompress those sections. And if those who are reading this right now only knew what the first draft looked like, they would thank you even more.

To the unsung heroes—all of the teachers and coaches in my life who invested far more in developing me than I deserved, and who were paid far less than they deserved for their constant sacrifices in such noble professions—thank you for your tireless dedication and passion for excellence. There are too many of you to name here, but on behalf of thousands of young men and women whom you've taught, guided, coached, and helped reach their potential in life, please know how indebted and grateful we are. While we can never adequately repay you, I hope we can honor your legacy by passing it on to others.

There is one coach I do need to call out, and that's Tommy Dixon—the toughest coach I ever had. Thank you for keeping fourteen players on your seventh grade basketball roster instead of thirteen, so I could be on your team. I must admit, though, I was elated when that season was over so I wouldn't have to suffer through another one of your practices. But then you kept getting promoted each year and somehow ended up as my basketball coach every season through high school. It must have been destiny, which I'm grateful for now. Thank you for teaching me the importance of perseverance through adversity and passion for personal improvement, which have been so valuable in my professional life and development as a leader.

To Colonel (Retired) Art Athens, thank you for inspiring me to be a Marine. Your leadership example and mentorship in my life for almost forty years since I was a midshipman at the Naval Academy have been instrumental in shaping me as a leader. Just as your influence has spanned every chapter of my leadership development journey, it also spans every chapter in this book. I am exceptionally blessed and grateful for the countless hours and energy you've invested in me over the years, and for the profound impact you've had in my life and thousands of others.

To all of the Marines I've had the privilege of knowing and serving with during my military career, thank you for helping me become a better person and teaching me how to lead. You set the example for me to learn from, and many of you carried me on your shoulders. I am forever grateful, and this book is dedicated to you. Semper Fidelis.

To Carey Lohrenz, thank you for introducing me to Clint Greenleaf and his extraordinary publishing team at Content Capital. I was flying blind, trying to figure out how to even begin publishing a book, and you took me on your wing to help lead me through the process. As a best-selling author with a full plate launching your second book, you didn't have to do that. But you did, and I'm extremely grateful for your guidance and confidence in my story.

To my publishing team at Content Capital—Clint Greenleaf, Whitney Gossett, and Lauren Hall—I couldn't have imagined a better experience or a better team to work with. Clint, thank you for giving me the opportunity, and for your inspiring professionalism and integrity. Whitney, thank you for your invaluable wisdom and guidance throughout my journey. And to my amazing editor, Lauren—thank you for your patience with this first-time author. You have such an empowering gift for shaping and sharpening the story, while enabling me to keep my own voice and ownership of the content. Thank you for investing your incredible talent and vast experience in me, and for pushing me to deliver the best book I'm capable of publishing. Whitney told me you are the best of the best when we started, and she was right.

To all of the accomplished leaders who were so generous in contributing endorsements to the book, thank you for your exceptionally kind and humbling words. I have tremendous respect and admiration for each of you, and I am extremely grateful for your leadership example, mentorship, and friendship over the years. The threads of your influence are woven throughout this book, in addition to the numerous lives you've each touched in such profound and impactful ways through your own distinctive leadership journeys. Thank you for making such a difference in my life and so many others.

Finally, I wouldn't have written this book if not for the immeasurable love and support of my family. To my wife, Mary Delle, thank you for your unwavering patience and untiring support during the seemingly endless COVID-19 weeks and weekends I spent in my office working on the manuscript, and for reading and editing so many drafts to help me say it better. More importantly, I wouldn't be the man or leader I am today without you. I love and appreciate you beyond words. To my adult children—Abbey, Drew, and Audrey—thank you for teaching me when you were younger that leadership starts at home, and for always forgiving me along the way when I failed. To this day, my most important mission and greatest blessing in life has been the opportunity to be your dad. Thank you for the joy it has been and continues to be. I love and admire you all, and I am so proud of the difference you are making in the world.

In conclusion, thank you for answering my self-doubt about whether anyone would actually read this book. Now I know it was all worth it. I hope it has resonated with you in some way. If it has, please pass it on in the way that you lead. And if it makes a difference in helping you reach your full potential as a leader, or in helping your team members reach their full potential as a team, I'd love to hear about it. Until then, best wishes in your journey leading your team to new heights!

APPENDIX

High-Performance Leadership Framework

Attract talent:
Create a *culture* that people want to be part of

Character • Competence • Composure

CULTURE

Develop talent:
Create an *environment* where *people* can grow

Respect
Know
Care

Retain talent:
Create a *mission* that people are inspired by

Prioritization
Preparation
Passion

COACH & DEVELOP

LEADER'S INTENT

PEOPLE

MISSION

INSPIRE & EMPOWER

Generate buy-in to the **leader**

Respect
Know
Care

INSPIRE

People are emotionally invested in mission success

Generate buy-in to the **mission**

Articulate
Reinforce
Illuminate

Involve your people in creating solutions

Ask for help
Ask how
Ask about hazards

EMPOWER

People have a sense of ownership for mission success

Support your people in executing solutions

Delegate
Debrief
Defend

The Leadership Triad

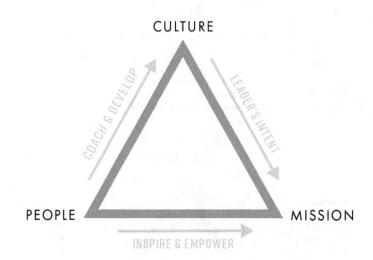

Outline for Creating a Leader's Intent

- Mission: task and purpose

    - Key question: "What does my team need to accomplish, and why?"

- Vision: a picture of a future end-state

    - Key question: "What does success look like for my team?"

- Values: important beliefs or ideals shared by the members of a group, which serve as broad guidelines in shaping the team's behaviors, attitudes, and culture

    - Key question: "What values will we hold ourselves accountable to?"

- Goals: observable and measurable results

    - Key question: "What is my team's primary goal over the next six months?"

- Priorities: things that merit the most attention among competing alternatives

    - Key question: "In order to achieve our goal, where will we need to focus our efforts and resources?"

- Expectations: standards of conduct and performance

    - Key questions: "What can my team expect from me as a leader, and what do I expect from them?"

Outline for Writing a Leader's Intent

"My team's mission is to _____, in order
to _____. We will know we are successful when __
_____. We will hold ourselves
accountable to the following values: _____
_____. Our primary goal over the next
six months is _____. In order
to achieve this goal, we will need to focus our efforts and resources in the following key areas: _____
___. As a leader, my team can expect the following from me: ___
_____. And I
expect the following from my team members: _____
_____."

Six Questions for Getting to Know People on Your Front Lines

1. *What's your name* (after introducing yourself, assuming you are meeting for the first time)?

2. *Where are you from?* People love to talk about where they are from, and many times there's an instant connection to someplace you've been or someone you know.

3. *Can you tell me about your family?* This is where their eyes usually light up.

4. *What do you love most about your job?* You can typically discern very quickly how inspired they are.

5. *What are your goals?* They will often be surprised that you asked and you will often be surprised that you can help, if only through a word of encouragement.

6. *What is your biggest challenge?* Most will be willing to share and many will be moved that you care. Often they will offer recommended solutions before you can ask, "If you were king for a day, what would you do to fix it?" The more conversations you have with people on the front lines of your organization, the more clearly you will be able to see patterns of problems emerging, along with good recommendations regarding how you can improve.

The "4 W's" of Effective Delegation

1. *Who*—choose the right person to delegate to considering their skills, experience, capacity, and level of interest . . . and your overall level of trust in their judgment and abilities
2. *Why*—explain the context and background behind what you need help with, and why it's important
3. *What*—summarize what needs to be accomplished, and what success looks like
4. *When*—if they are willing and able to help, align on an acceptable timeline that works for both of you, including intermediate milestones and a check-in cadence

Effective Coaching Mindset

MINDSET

An *encouraging* **TEACHER** that inspires *courage* and *confidence*

- **T**EACHABILITY
- **E**NTHUSIASM
- **A**PPROACHABILITY
- **C**REDIBILITY
- **H**UMILITY
- **E**MPATHY
- **R**ECEPTIVENESS

- Teachability: do you set the example in being teachable yourself?
- Enthusiasm: do you bring positive energy that is a catalyst for learning?
- Approachability: do you carry yourself in a way that causes others to feel comfortable sharing their challenges with you?
- Credibility: do you know your stuff and lead by example so that people trust and respect your advice?
- Humility: do you admit your mistakes and learn from them, so that others are willing to do the same?
- Empathy: do you put yourself in others' shoes and attempt to see things from their perspective?
- Receptiveness: do you seek to listen and understand before you speak and share your opinions?

Effective Coaching Method

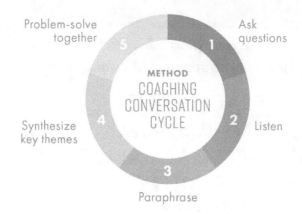

COACHING SUCCESS FORMULA

Compassionate **+** Candid **+** Confidential **= TRUST**

Practical Steps for Conducting a Difficult Conversation

1. Focus on having a learning conversation—explore, ask questions, and listen (listening can transform a conversation and helps the other person listen to you)
2. Set the right tone—ground the conversation up front by acknowledging the other person's value and feelings (show empathy)
3. Frame the issue by sharing its impact on you, others, and/or the organization (decouple this from any perceptions you may have regarding intentions)
4. Ask about their intentions (don't assume, since assumptions about intentions are often wrong)
5. Focus on issues, not personalities
6. Look for common ground
7. Reflect before you speak, and paraphrase for clarity
8. Problem-solve together
9. Be flexible and adjust expectations based on how the conversation evolves
10. Agree to next steps and establish a feedback loop

Myers-Briggs Type Indicator (MBTI) Personality Assessment

The Myers-Briggs Type Indicator (MBTI) personality assessment is designed to show psychological tendencies in how people view the world and make decisions. It was developed by Katharine Briggs and her daughter Isabel Briggs Myers in the 1940s through research based on Swiss psychiatrist Carl Jung's theory that people engage with their environment using four key psychological domains: introversion vs. extraversion, sensing vs. intuition, thinking vs. feeling, and judging vs. perception. The MBTI is used by more than 10,000 companies, 2,500 colleges and universities, and 200 government agencies in the United States. You can complete a free assessment in less than ten minutes at the following web address: https://www.16personalities.com/.

Four Steps to Improve Your Prioritization and Time Management

1. Assess—understand how you *currently* spend your time
2. Aspire—determine how you *want* to spend your time
3. Address—identify what needs to *change*
4. Act—decide *how* to implement desired changes and take appropriate steps

TIME MANAGEMENT ASSESSMENT CATEGORIES

- Sleep
- Food / meals
- Workout / exercise
- Life / personal / home / family / social
- Commute / travel
- Meetings
- E-mail / communication / administration
- Hiring / interviews
- Direct reports
- Boss
- Projects / tasks / research
- Thinking / strategy / reading
- Unplanned issues / opportunities (i.e., "pop-ups")
- Relationships (work-related)
- Other (unique to an individual or industry)

EXAMPLE TIME MANAGEMENT ASSESSMENT SPREADSHEET

TIME MANAGEMENT ASSESSMENT						
Categories	Time block	Mon	Tue	Wed	Thr	Fri
(S) Sleep	0000-0100					
(F) Food/meals	0100-0200					
(W) Workout/exercise	0200-0300					
(L) Life/personal/home/family/social	0300-0400					
(C) Commute/travel	0400-0500					
(M) Meetings	0500-0600					
(E) E-mail/communication/administration	0600-0700					
(H) Hiring/interviews	0700-0800					
(D) Direct reports	0800-0900					
(B) Boss	0900-1000					
(P) Projects/tasks/research	1000-1100					
(T) Thinking/strategy/reading	1100-1200					
(U) Unplanned issues/opportunities	1200-1300					
(R) Relationships (work-related)	1300-1400					
(O) Other	1400-1500					
	1500-1600					
	1600-1700					
	1700-1800					
	1800-1900					
	1900-2000					
	2000-2100					
	2100-2200					
	2200-2300					
	2300-2400					

Five Steps for Running an Efficient and Effective Meeting

1. PREPARE

Start with the purpose. If you can't identify the purpose of the meeting, you shouldn't have it. Then think through your desired outcomes. Next, put together an agenda that includes a list of topics, the time allocated for each topic, and who will lead the discussion for each topic if applicable. Thoughtfully create a list of attendees based on the topics you plan to cover, and separate them into required versus optional. Finally, send out a calendar invite with plenty of lead time that succinctly outlines the purpose, desired outcomes, and agenda. Put required attendees in the "To" line and optional attendees in the "CC" line, and attach any appropriate read-ahead materials.

2. LEAD

Start on time, even if everyone isn't on time. Establish ground rules or "rules of engagement" for the meeting. These might include starting and ending on time, asking for everyone's participation and encouraging a healthy debate, agreeing to listen to others and limit interruptions, clarifying how decisions will be made, and establishing a multi-tasking policy. Be the tone-setter and focus on effectively facilitating the discussion by drawing equitably on everyone's perspectives. Stick to the agenda and manage time efficiently. This might involve using a "parking lot" for issues to be discussed and dealt with later. Take notes to record important ideas, key points, and decisions.

3. CLOSE

Focus on concluding with the right tone and clarifying expectations so that attendees are motivated to follow through. Summarize the session. Reiterate key points, decisions, next steps, and who is responsible for what by when. Ask if there are any final questions, comments, or concerns. Finish on a positive note, even if it's as simple as, "Great discussion today, thank you!"

4. FOLLOW UP

Send an e-mail to all of the participants to document the results of the meeting. Start with the date, purpose, agenda, and attendees. Provide a brief summary of key discussion points. Highlight specific outcomes or decisions. Reinforce accountability by listing the agreed-upon next steps, including who is responsible for what by when.

5. ASK FOR FEEDBACK

Request a quick debrief with one or two participants from the meeting. This could be someone whom you respect and trust to give you candid feedback. Or it might be someone who seemed "difficult" during the meeting. In either case, ask for an opportunity to meet one-on-one at their convenience to discuss what you can do to improve the effectiveness of your meetings.

Leading Through Uncertainty

COLLABORATIVE PLANNING PROCESS

STEP	DESCRIPTION
1. LEADER'S GUIDANCE	Mission: *What, Why, Success Criteria* (Task, Purpose, End-state)
2. MISSION ANALYSIS	Planning factors: "CRAFT" • *Competition, Resources, Atmospherics* (e.g., social, cultural, political, regulatory), *Functions* (expertise needed for planning and execution), *Time*
3. COA DEVELOPMENT	Course of Action (COA): *What* needs to be done, by *When*, by *Whom* • *Cross-functional, task-organized team*
4. CONTINGENCY PLANNING	• What could go wrong (risks)? What could go unexpectedly well (opportunities)? • How will you know that these risks/opportunities are developing (critical information triggers)? • What will you do about them (contingency responses)?
5. DECISION	• At least two COAs for the decision-maker to choose from (or combine) • Brief the Mission Analysis, COA overview, key contingency plans, pros/cons assessment
6. EXECUTION	Clearly communicate initially to the execution team, and iteratively as required: • *Leader's Guidance, Mission Analysis* (mission and context) • *Execution team roles and responsibilities* (who does what when, contingency responses)
7. DEBRIEF	Focus on continuous improvement for the planning and execution team(s) • *Performance* (results vs. objectives) • *Process*

Deliberate Decision-Making Checklist

1. Is this a decision that I need to make now?
2. Did I consider the strategic context, including realistic constraints?
3. Did I get the right people with the right expertise in the room?
4. Did I accurately frame the issue and encourage rigorous debate?
5. Did I collect all of the relevant facts and consider all aspects of the issue?
6. Did I identify and appropriately weigh the risks and opportunities?
7. Do I feel enough conviction to be decisive and explain *why* I made the decision?

Leading Operational Change

PROBLEM-SOLVING PROCESS

STEP	DESCRIPTION	COMMENTS
1	DEFINE THE PROBLEM	Clearly articulate and align on the answer to, "What problem are we trying to solve?"
2	DISSECT THE PROBLEM	Identify the key issues
3	PRIORITIZE KEY ISSUES	Which questions are most critical, and which ones are likely less important?
4	PLAN YOUR RESEARCH	Think efficiency (time and resources)
5	CONDUCT RESEARCH & ANALYSIS	Think 80-20 rule
6	SYNTHESIZE YOUR FINDINGS	What is the "so what"? (i.e., what practical actions are implied by the findings)
7	PROPOSE YOUR SOLUTION	Answer to the question, "What should we do?" (think clarity and impact)

Leading Organizational Change

SEVEN STEPS TO CREATE AND SUSTAIN CHANGE

STEP	DESCRIPTION
1	Create a compelling case for change (a "burning platform" where people believe you must do something)
2	Initiate strategic communication from the top including the purpose and importance of the effort, and what success looks like (change vision)
3	Recruit key influencers to join your transformation team, and collaboratively develop a strategy to achieve the vision (generate buy-in)
4	Engage line-level stakeholders to create "champions" by helping them understand the importance of the effort and what's in it for them
5	Celebrate quick wins for momentum
6	Implement a high-visibility reporting cadence with top leadership
7	Embed results in organizational systems and culture for sustainability

Leading Through a Crisis

1. RAPIDLY ANALYZE THE SITUATION

Huddle with your senior leadership team, including legal and public relations. Also bring into the conversation anyone who has a good grasp of the facts surrounding the crisis. Avoid the temptation to jump to conclusions or prematurely place blame. Focus on what happened, given what you currently know, what the implications and impacts are for people within and external to your organization, and what immediate actions you can take to help stem the crisis and mitigate further damage. Once aligned, initiate the immediate actions.

2. SHAPE YOUR COMMUNICATIONS

Focus on honesty and empathy. The key is to develop trust with people inside and outside your organization by taking responsibility, telling the truth, and acknowledging the emotional challenges people are experiencing as a result of the crisis. Develop a concise message that describes what happened, empathetically acknowledges the impact, and explains what you are doing about it. Do all of this quickly so you can drive the narrative, rather than react to it. Remember that bad news rarely, if ever, gets better with time.

3. EXERCISE VISIBLE LEADERSHIP

Step into the spotlight and be ready to take the heat for your team. This is far from comfortable, but it's one of the most important things you'll ever do as a leader. Remember our discussion about composure as it relates to your culture in chapter 1? This is your chance to let your true character shine in the face of real adversity. Start by sharing your message with your team and offer them the opportunity to ask questions. Instruct them to refer any media inquiries to your senior leadership team, because your next step is to deliver the same message to people outside your organization through a press release, press conference, video interview, social media, and/or other appropriate communication channels. Conclude by announcing that you've commenced an investigation (we'll talk about this in a second), and will update everyone as you learn more. Throughout this entire process, keep reminding yourself that accountability and transparency are your keys to developing trust.

4. CREATE A CRISIS ACTION TEAM

Carefully consider the expertise needed based on the nature of the crisis, and ensure the team has adequate information flow to create a data-driven, fact-based common operating picture. Use the *Collaborative Planning Process* that we previously discussed to rapidly generate potential courses of action. Begin by assessing the results of your immediate actions, and adjust next steps accordingly. Accelerate and iterate your COA decision cycle to stay ahead of the crisis, and make sure you have a plan to stay ahead of the media.

5. INITIATE AN INVESTIGATION

As soon as the crisis begins to stabilize, commence an investigation. Depending on the nature of the crisis, the investigation can be conducted formally or informally by an internal or external body. When deciding among these options, weigh the importance of resource intensity and speed versus the perception of objectivity and integrity. For example, an informal investigation conducted internally might be the fastest way to generate insights, but this may also increase the risk of cover-up allegations. On the other hand, a formal investigation by an external third party may be more thorough and objective, but this could also result in delayed insights, making it harder for you to stay ahead of the media. Consider balancing these risks by launching an informal, internal investigation to generate rapid initial insights, followed immediately by a formal, external investigation. Thoughtfully assess the expertise you need on the investigating team in order to ensure rigor and accuracy in the findings. Results of the investigation should address, at a minimum, two things: cause(s), and recommendations for how to prevent a similar crisis from occurring in the future. Use these findings to update your internal and external communications. Own your mistakes, vow to do better, and put into place measures for continuous improvement within your organization.

The Influence Pyramid

A PRACTICAL FRAMEWORK FOR
LEADING THROUGH INFLUENCE

DEPENDABILITY	Follow through: be reliable, responsive, and results-oriented
EXPERTISE	Demonstrate the value of your knowledge, experience, and network
RESPECT	Be inclusive, use "we" instead of "I," value others' opinions, be influenceable yourself
CONTEXT	Talk about the big picture and the broader good, generate alignment through vision
CONNECTION	Start by building relationships, identify shared interests, find common ground

NOTES

Chapter 1: Culture

1. IMDb, "Awards: Louis Gossett Jr.," https://www.imdb.com/name/nm0001283/awards.

2. Robert Frost, "The Road Not Taken," in *Mountain Interval* (New York: Henry Holt and Company, 1916), 9–10.

3. Dale Wimbrow, "The Guy in the Glass," 1934, https://www.theguyintheglass.com/gig.htm.

Chapter 2: People

4. United States Army, Medal of Honor citation for Private William J. Crawford, May 30, 1984, https://www.cmohs.org/recipients/william-j-crawford.

5. Colonel James Moschgat, United States Air Force, "Lessons in Leadership: From a Janitor," *Wharton Leadership Digest*, December 2001, http://www.pnbhs.school.nz/wp-content/uploads/2015/11/Lessons-in-Leadership-from-a-Janitor.pdf.

6. The Nielson Company, "U.S. Consumers Are Shifting the Time They Spend with Media," March 19, 2019, https://www.nielsen.com/us/en/insights/article/2019/us-consumers-are-shifting-the-time-they-spend-with-media/.

Chapter 3: Mission

7. National Aeronautics and Space Administration, "Fred Haise—Native-Son-Turned-Enduring-Hero," April 15, 2020, https://www.nasa.gov/centers/stennis/news/press-release/2020/Fred-Haise-Native-Son-Turned-Enduring-Hero; Elizabeth Howell and Kimberly Hickok, "Jack Swigert: Apollo 13 Command Module Pilot," *Space*, April 8, 2020, https://www.space.com/20319-jack-swigert-apollo-13-biography.html; National Aeronautics and Space Administration Biographical Data, "James A. Lovell (Captain, USN, Ret.)," December 1994, https://www.nasa.gov/sites/default/files/atoms/files/lovell_james_0.pdf.

8. National Aeronautics and Space Administration, *Apollo Program Summary Report* (April 1975), 466, https://www.hq.nasa.gov/alsj/APSR-JSC-09423-OCR.pdf; Smithsonian National Air and Space Museum, "Apollo 13 (AS-508)," https://airandspace.si.edu/explore-and-learn/topics/apollo/apollo-program/landing-missions/apollo13.cfm.

9. National Aeronautics and Space Administration, *Apollo 13 Press Kit* (April 2, 1970), 104, https://history.nasa.gov/alsj/a13/A13_PressKit.pdf; James Lovell, "Houston, We've Had a Problem," in *Apollo Expeditions to the Moon*, chap. 13, https://history.nasa.gov/SP-350/ch-13-1.html.

10. National Aeronautics and Space Administration, "Apollo 13," July 8, 2009, https://www.nasa.gov/mission_pages/apollo/missions/apollo13.html.

11. National Aeronautics and Space Administration, "Biography: Gene Kranz—A Blast From the Past," https://www.nasa.gov/sites/default/files/files/Gene-Kranz-Bio.pdf; Stephen Cass, "Apollo 13, We Have a Solution," *Spectrum*, April 1, 2005, https://spectrum.ieee.org/tech-history/space-age/apollo-13-we-have-a-solution; Solar System Exploration Research Virtual Institute, "Apollo 13 Commander Remembers the Aborted Moon Mission," https://sservi.nasa.gov/articles/apollo-13-commander-remembers-the-aborted-moon-mission/.

12. Cass, "Apollo 13, We Have a Solution"; National Aeronautics and Space Administration, *Apollo 13 Mission Report* (September 1, 1970), 3-3 to 3-4, https://ntrs.nasa.gov/citations/19710003598.

13. *Magnolia State Live*, "Mississippi Moonshot: Jerry Bostic, Flight Dynamics Officer That Inadvertently Created Famous 'Apollo 13' Line," July 19, 2019, https://www.magnoliastatelive.com/2019/07/19/mississippi-moonshot-jerry-bostick-flight-dynamics-officer-that-inadvertently-created-famous-apollo-13-line/.

14. Attributed to Canadian IT professional Simon Fulleringer.

15. John Wooden with Jack Tobin, *They Call Me Coach* (New York: McGraw-Hill, 1972).

16. John Wooden with Steve Jamison, *Wooden: A Lifetime of Observations and Reflections On and Off the Court* (New York: McGraw-Hill, 1997), 108.

Chapter 4: Connecting Culture to Mission Through Your Leader's Intent

17. Elbert Hubbard, *A Message to Garcia* (USA: Seven Treasures Publications, 2009); American Film Institute, *Catalog of Feature Films*, "A Message to Garcia," April 10, 1936, https://catalog.afi.com/Catalog/moviedetails/3908.

18. Colonel Andrew Rowan, United States Army, "How I Carried the Message to Garcia," *Foundations Magazine*, http://www.foundationsmag.com/rowan.html; "Spanish-American War," *History*, last updated February 21, 2020, https://www.history.com/topics/early-20th-century-us/spanish-american-war.

19. Hubbard, *A Message to Garcia*.

20. Ibid.; Rowan, "How I Carried the Message to Garcia."

21. Hubbard, *A Message to Garcia*.

22. Smithsonian National Air and Space Museum, "The Moon Decision," https://airandspace.si.edu/exhibitions/apollo-to-the-moon/online/racing-to-space/moon-decision.cfm#:~:text=On%20May%2025%2C%201961%2C%20he,the%20end%20of%20the%20decade; Charles Fishman, "This 46-Minute John F. Kennedy Speech Reshaped the History of Space Exploration (and It Almost Didn't Happen)," Fast Company, June 2, 2019, https://www.fastcompany.com/90357583/this-46-minute-john-f-kennedy-speech-reshaped-the-history-of-space-exploration#:~:text=The%20speech%2C%20which%20White%20House,last%2Dminute%20change%20of%20heart.

23. Olivia Waxman, "Lots of People Have Theories about Neil Armstrong's 'One Small Step for Man' Quote. Here's What We Really Know," Time, July 15, 2019, https://time.com/5621999/neil-armstrong-quote/.

24. U.S. Army Heritage and Education Center, "Who First Originated the Term VUCA (Volatility, Uncertainty, Complexity and Ambiguity)?" May 7, 2019, https://usawc.libanswers.com/friendly.php?slug=faq/84869.

25. Simon Sinek, Start with Why: How Great Leaders Inspire Everyone to Take Action (New York: Portfolio / Penguin, 2009).

26. General David Berger, United States Marine Corps, "A Message from the Commandant of the Marine Corps," Marine Corps Gazette, November 2020, www.mca-marines.org/gazette.

Chapter 5: Connecting People to Mission by Inspiring and Empowering Your Team

27. Chris Roush, Inside Home Depot (New York: McGraw Hill, 1999), 1–8; The Home Depot, "The Home Is Where Our Story Begins," https://corporate.homedepot.com/about/history.

28. Bernie Marcus and Arthur Blank, Built from Scratch: How a Couple of Regular Guys Grew The Home Depot from Nothing to $30 Billion (New York: Crown Business, 1999), 104, 270, Kindle.

29. The Home Depot, Annual Report 2019, https://ir.homedepot.com/~/media/Files/H/HomeDepot-IR/2020/2019_THD_AnnualReport_vf.pdf; PricewaterhouseCoopers (PwC), "Global Top 100 Companies by Market Capitalisation," June 30, 2020, https://www.pwc.com/gx/en/audit-services/publications/assets/global-top-100-companies-june-2020-update.pdf.

30. John Maxwell, The 21 Irrefutable Laws of Leadership (Nashville, TN: Thomas Nelson, Inc., 1998), 99.

31. Theodore Roosevelt, Goodreads, https://www.goodreads.com/quotes/34690-people-don-t-care-how-much-you-know-until-they-know.

32. John Girard and Sandra Lambert, "The Story of Knowledge: Writing Stories that Guide Organisations into the Future," The Electronic Journal of Knowledge Management 5 no. 2 (2007): 161, https://academic-publishing.org/index.php/ejkm/article/view/769.

33. Nancy Duarte and Patti Sanchez, Illuminate: Ignite Change Through Speeches, Stories, Ceremonies, and Symbols (New York: Portfolio / Penguin, 2016).

34. Victor Lipman, "Why Do Employees Leave Their Jobs? New Survey Offers Answers," *Forbes*, October 10, 2015, https://www.forbes.com/sites/victorlipman/2015/10/10/why-do-employees-leave-their-jobs-new-survey-offers-answers/#1a4e0957ea15; Ifeoma Obi, "The Effects of the Micromanagement of the Staff on the Business," *The Human Capital Hub*, July 15, 2020, https://www.thehumancapitalhub.com/articles/The-Effects-Of-The-Micromanagement-Of-Staff-On-The-Business.

35. Jesse Sostrin, "To Be a Great Leader, You Have to Learn How to Delegate Well," *Harvard Business Review*, October 10, 2017, https://hbr.org/2017/10/to-be-a-great-leader-you-have-to-learn-how-to-delegate-well.

36. Harvard Business School Publishing, *Delegating Work* (Boston: Harvard Business Review Press, 2014), 22–28.

37. Simon Sinek, *Leaders Eat Last: Why Some Teams Pull Together and Others Don't* (New York: Portfolio / Penguin, 2014), 49, Kindle.

38. *Delegating Work*, 6–9.

39. Iskandar Aminov, Aaron De Smet, Gregor Jost, and David Mendelsohn, "Decision Making in the Age of Urgency," *McKinsey & Company*, April 30, 2019, https://www.mckinsey.com/business-functions/organization/our-insights/decision-making-in-the-age-of-urgency.

Chapter 6: Connecting People to Culture by Coaching and Developing Your Team

40. Google, "From the Garage to the Googleplex," https://about.google/our-story/; Google, "Our Mission," https://www.google.com/search/howsearchworks/mission/.

41. David Garvin, Alison Wagonfeld, and Liz Kind, *Google's Project Oxygen: Do Managers Matter?* (Boston: Harvard Business School Publishing, 2013); Jonathan Strickland, "How the Googleplex Works," *HowStuffWorks*, August 4, 2008, https://computer.howstuffworks.com/googleplex.htm.

42. Garvin, Wagonfeld, and Kind, *Google's Project Oxygen: Do Managers Matter?*

43. Ibid.

44. Ibid.

45. Monique Valcour, "You Can't Be a Great Manager If You're Not a Good Coach," *Harvard Business Review*, July 17, 2014, https://hbr.org/2014/07/you-cant-be-a-great-manager-if-youre-not-a-good-coach.

46. Rebecca Knight, "How to Make Your One-on-Ones with Employees More Productive," *Harvard Business Review*, August 8, 2016, https://hbr.org/2016/08/how-to-make-your-one-on-ones-with-employees-more-productive.

47. Ibid.

48. Rich Lyons, "Feedback: You Need to Lead It," *Forbes*, July 10, 2017, https://www.forbes.com/sites/richlyons/2017/07/10/feedback-you-need-to-lead-it/#65e512494a35.

49. Harvard Business School Publishing, *Giving Effective Feedback* (Boston: Harvard Business Review Press, 2014), 8–9.

50. Ibid., 14.

51. Ibid., 15–16.

52. Ibid., 20–21; Marcial Losada and Emily Heaphy, "The Role of Positivity and Connectivity in the Performance of Business Teams: A Nonlinear Dynamics Model," *American Behavioral Scientist* 47, no. 6 (February 1, 2004): 740–65, https://journals.sagepub.com/doi/abs/10.1177/0002764203260208.

53. *Giving Effective Feedback*, 7, 27–48.

54. Ibid., 18.

55. Ibid., 52.

56. Michael Schneider, "Most People Handle Difficult Situations by Ignoring Them—and the Fallout Isn't Pretty," *Inc.*, August 22, 2018, https://www.inc.com/michael-schneider/70-percent-of-employees-avoid-difficult-conversations-their-companies-are-suffering-as-a-result.html.

57. Tracey Powley, "Having Your First 'Difficult' Conversation," *The Institute of Leadership and Management*, https://www.institutelm.com/resourceLibrary/having-your-first--difficult--conversation.html#:~:text=A%20survey%20conducted%20by%20the,with%20their%20team%20at%20work.&text=Clearly%2C%20we%20need%20to%20be,within%20their%20teams%20at%20work.

58. Joann Lublin, "The High Cost of Avoiding Conflict at Work," *Wall Street Journal*, February 14, 2014, https://www.wsj.com/articles/SB10001424052702304315004579382780060647804; Schneider, "Most People Handle Difficult Situations by Ignoring Them—and the Fallout Isn't Pretty."

59. Harvard Business School Publishing, *Difficult Conversations* (Boston: Harvard Business Review Press, 2016), 5–13.

60. Ibid., 18–20.

61. Judith Glaser and Richard Glaser, "The Neurochemistry of Positive Conversations," *Harvard Business Review*, June 12, 2014, https://hbr.org/2014/06/the-neurochemistry-of-positive-conversations; Douglas Stone, Bruce Patton, and Sheila Heen, *Difficult Conversations: How to Discuss What Matters Most* (New York: Penguin, 1999); Daniel Goleman, *Emotional Intelligence* (New York: Bantam, 1995); Allison Rimm, "To Guide Difficult Conversations, Try Using Compassion," *Harvard Business Review*, June 19, 2013, https://hbr.org/2013/06/to-guide-difficult-conversatio; Harvard Business School Publishing, *Difficult Conversations*, 41–42.

62. Glaser and Glaser, "The Neurochemistry of Positive Conversations."

63. Ibid.

64. Ibid.

65. Stone, Patton, and Heen, *Difficult Conversations*; Harvard Business School Publishing, *Difficult Conversations*, 49–68.

66. Bojana Jokanovic, Ivana Tomic, and Ljubica Dudak, "Organizational Conflict Resolution," International Scientific Conference on Industrial Systems, October 4, 2017, https://www.iim.ftn.uns.ac.rs/is17/papers/81.pdf.

67. Franny Spengler and Dirk Scheele, "Oxytocin Facilitates Reciprocity in Social Communication," *Social Cognitive and Affective Neuroscience* 12, no. 8 (August 2017): 1325–33, https://www.ncbi.nlm.nih.gov/pmc/articles/PMC5597889/.

68. Amy Gallo, *Guide to Dealing with Conflict* (Boston: Harvard Business Press, 2017), 15–25.

69. Ibid., xxi–xxii.

70. Amy Edmondson, *The Fearless Organization: Creating Psychological Safety in the Workplace for Learning, Innovation, and Growth* (Hoboken, NJ: Wiley, 2019); Lauren Johnson, "How to Encourage Healthy Conflict," *Harvard Business Review*, August 1, 2008, https://hbsp.harvard.edu/product/U0808B-PDF-ENG?itemFindingMethod=Other.

71. Gallo, *Guide to Dealing with Conflict*, 3–13.

72. Ibid., 31–40.

73. Ibid., 61–98.

74. Jokanovic, Tomic, and Dudak, "Organizational Conflict Resolution."

75. Ralph Kilmann and Kenneth Thomas, "Developing a Forced-Choice Measure of Conflict-Handling Behavior: The 'Mode' Instrument," *Education and Psychological Measurement* 37, no. 2 (July 1977): 309–25, https://journals.sagepub.com/doi/10.1177/001316447703700204.

76. Gallo, *Guide to Dealing with Conflict*, 101–3.

77. Liane Davey, "Conflict Strategies for Nice People," *Harvard Business Review*, December 25, 2013, https://hbr.org/2013/12/conflict-strategies-for-nice-people.

78. James Grinnell, *Leadership, Management, and Coaching* (New York: Vilnius Press, 2012), 17.

Chapter 7: Balancing the Essentials to Maximize Your Leadership Effectiveness

79. Randy Cordle, "Project: Three-Legged Stool," https://www.highlandwoodworking.com/woodworking-projects/three-legged-stool-woodworking-project.html.

80. Isabel Briggs Myers with Peter Briggs Myers, *Gifts Differing: Understanding Personality Type* (Mountain View, CA: Davies-Black Publishing, 1995), xi–9.

81. Lillian Cunningham, "Myers-Briggs: Does It Pay to Know Your Type?" *Washington Post*, December 14, 2012, https://www.washingtonpost.com/national/on-leadership/myers-briggs-does-it-pay-to-know-your-type/2012/12/14/eaed51ae-3fcc-11e2-bca3-aadc9b7e29c5_story.html.

82. Pablo Picasso, *Goodreads*, https://www.goodreads.com/quotes/163897-art-is-the-elimination-of-the-unnecessary.

83. A. L. Williams, *All You Can Do Is All You Can Do* (Nashville: Oliver-Nelson, 1988).

84. Stephen Covey, *First Things First* (Miami: Mango Media, 2015), 97–98, Kindle.

85. Charles Hummel, *Tyranny of the Urgent* (Downers Grove, IL: InterVarsity Press, 1994).

86. Leslie Perlow, Constance Hadley, and Eunice Eun, "Stop the Meeting Madness," *Harvard Business Review*, July-August 2017, https://hbr.org/2017/07/stop-the-meeting-madness.

87. Harvard Business School Publishing, *Running Meetings* (Boston: Harvard Business Review Press, 2014), 9–71.

88. Peter Bregman, "The Magic of 30-Minute Meetings," *Harvard Business Review*, February 22, 2016, https://hbr.org/2016/02/the-magic-of-30-minute-meetings.

89. C. Northcote Parkinson, "Parkinson's Law," *The Economist*, November 19, 1955, https://www.economist.com/news/1955/11/19/parkinsons-law, actual quote: "Work expands so as to fill the time available for its completion."

Chapter 8: Adapting the Essentials to Lead Through Uncertainty and Change

90. Declan Butler, "A World Where Everyone Has a Robot: Why 2040 Could Blow Your Mind," *Nature*, February 24, 2016, https://www.nature.com/news/a-world-where-everyone-has-a-robot-why-2040-could-blow-your-mind-1.19431.

91. IBM, "10 Key Marketing Trends for 2017," *IBM Marketing Cloud*, ftp://ftp.www.ibm.com/software/in/pdf/10_Key_Marketing_Trends_for_2017.pdf; John Gantz and David Reinsel, "The Digital Universe in 2020," *IDC IVIEW*, December 2012, https://www.cs.princeton.edu/courses/archive/spring13/cos598C/idc-the-digital-universe-in-2020.pdf.

92. "The Perils of Prediction," *The Economist*, May 31, 2007, https://www.economist.com/books-and-arts/2007/05/31/the-perils-of-prediction; Nate Scott, "The 50 Greatest Yogi Berra Quotes," *USA Today*, March 28, 2019, https://ftw.usatoday.com/2019/03/the-50-greatest-yogi-berra-quotes.

93. "TED Speaker: Alan Kay—Educator and Computing Pioneer," *TED*, March 2008, https://www.ted.com/speakers/alan_kay.

94. William Blair, "President Draws Planning Moral: Recalls Army Days to Show Value of Preparedness in Time of Crisis," *New York Times*, November 15, 1957, https://www.nytimes.com/1957/11/15/archives/president-draws-planning-moral-recalls-army-days-to-show-value-of.html.

95. Helmuth von Moltke, quoted in Robert Heinl, *Dictionary of Military and Naval Quotations* (Annapolis, MD: Naval Institute Press, 1966), "Plans," Kindle.

96. United States Army, *Field Manual 101-5: Staff Organization and Operations* (Washington, DC: Headquarters, Department of the Army, 1997), https://www.globalsecurity.org/military/library/policy/army/fm/101-5/f540.pdf.

97. Scott, "The 50 Greatest Yogi Berra Quotes."

98. National D-Day Memorial Foundation, "Preparation and Planning," https://www.dday.org/preparation-and-planning/.

99. Andrew Likierman, "The Elements of Good Judgment," *Harvard Business Review*, January-February 2020, https://hbr.org/2020/01/the-elements-of-good-judgment.

100. Daniel Kahneman, *Thinking Fast and Slow* (New York: Farrar, Straus and Giroux, 2011).

101. Suzanne Massie, *Trust, but Verify: Reagan, Russia, and Me* (Blue Hill, ME: Maine Authors Publishing, 2013).

102. Adapted from *Bulletproof Problem Solving: The One Skill That Changes Everything*, Charles Conn and Robert McLean (Hoboken, NJ: John Wiley & Sons, Inc., 2018) and "How to Master the Seven-Step Problem-Solving Process," McKinsey & Company, 13 September 2019, https://www.mckinsey.com/business-functions/strategy-and-corporate-finance/our-insights/how-to-master-the-seven-step-problem-solving-process.

103. William Craig, "Accepting Change Is Vital to Your Company's Growth," *Forbes*, November 13, 2017, https://www.forbes.com/sites/williamcraig/2017/11/13/accepting-change-is-vital-to-your-companys-growth/#516e39ae2b00.

104. John Kotter, "Accelerate!" *Harvard Business Review*, November, 2012, https://hbr.org/2012/11/accelerate; John Kotter, "Leading Change: Why Transformation Efforts Fail," *Harvard Business Review*, May-June, 1995, https://hbr.org/1995/05/leading-change-why-transformation-efforts-fail-2; John Kotter, *Leading Change* (Boston, MA: Harvard Business Review Press, 2012).

105. W. Chan Kim and Renee Mauborgne, "Tipping Point Leadership," *Harvard Business Review*, April 2003, https://hbr.org/2003/04/tipping-point-leadership; Robert Kegan and Lisa Lahey, "The Real Reason People Won't Change," *Harvard Business Review*, November 2001, https://hbr.org/2001/11/the-real-reason-people-wont-change.

106. Ed Catmull, *Creativity, Inc.* (New York: Random House, 2014), 85–128.

107. Peter Drucker, "The Discipline of Innovation," *Harvard Business Review*, August 2002, https://hbr.org/2002/08/the-discipline-of-innovation.

108. Linda Hill, Greg Brandeau, Emily Truelove, and Kent Lineback, *Collective Genius: The Art and Practice of Leading Innovation* (Boston: Harvard Business Review Press, 2014), Introduction, Kindle.

109. Ibid., chap. 4–5.

110. Kotter, *Leading Change*, chap. 1.

111. Theodore Roosevelt, "Citizenship in a Republic and the Man in the Arena: Speech at the Sorbonne, Paris, April 23, 1910," Kindle.

112. Barry Bloom, "Yogi Was Military Hero Before a Baseball Star," *MLB.com*, September 23, 2015, https://www.mlb.com/news/yogi-berra-had-decorated-military-career-too/c-151195348; "Yogi Berra Was at D-Day," interview with Keith Olbermann, *NBC News*, June 14, 2004, https://www.nbcnews.com/id/wbna5210564.

Chapter 9: Leveraging the Essentials to Lead Through Influence

113. Admiral James A. Winnefeld Jr., United States Navy (Retired), "A Letter in a Hat," *Shipmate*, June 2019.

114. Aristotle, *Rhetoric* (New York: Cosimo, 2010), 6–12.

115. Carmine Gallo, "The Art of Persuasion Hasn't Changed in 2,000 Years," *Harvard Business Review*, July 15, 2019, https://hbr.org/2019/07/the-art-of-persuasion-hasnt-changed-in-2000-years.

116. Ibid.

117. Ibid.

118. Ibid.

119. Robert Cialdini, "Harnessing the Science of Persuasion," *Harvard Business Review*, October 2001, https://hbr.org/2001/10/harnessing-the-science-of-persuasion; Robert Cialdini, *Influence: The Psychology of Persuasion* (New York: HarperCollins, 2009).

120. Tim Riesterer, "Stimulate Your Customer's Lizard Brain to Make a Sale," *Harvard Business Review*, July 31, 2012, https://hbr.org/2012/07/stimulate-your-customers-lizar.

121. Judith Glaser, "Your Brain Is Hooked on Being Right," *Harvard Business Review*, February 28, 2013, https://hbr.org/2013/02/break-your-addiction-to-being.

122. Edmondson, *The Fearless Organization*.

123. Google, "Guide: Understand Team Effectiveness," *re:Work*, https://rework.withgoogle.com/print/guides/5721312655835136/.

124. Riesterer, "Stimulate Your Customer's Lizard Brain to Make a Sale."

125. Adam Grant, "Persuading the Unpersuadable: Lessons from Science—and the People Who Were Able to Sway Steve Jobs," *Harvard Business Review*, March–April, 2021, https://hbr.org/2021/03/persuading-the-unpersuadable.

126. Ibid.; Dave Roos, "Steve Jobs Originally Envisioned the iPhone as Mostly a Phone," *History*, updated January 7, 2020, https://www.history.com/news/iphone-original-size-invention-steve-jobs; Jessica Bursztynsky, "Apple Surpasses Saudi Aramco to Become World's Most Valuable Company," *CNBC*, updated September 1, 2020, https://www.cnbc.com/2020/07/31/apple-surpasses-saudi-aramco-to-become-worlds-most-valuable-company.html.

127. Grant, "Persuading the Unpersuadable."

128. Ibid.

129. Ibid.

130. Discussions with Foghorn Therapeutics staff, Cambridge, MA, June 2019.

Conclusion

131. Steve Ewing and John Lundstrom, *Fateful Rendezvous: The Life of Butch O'Hare* (Annapolis, MD: Naval Institute Press, 1997), 1–155, Kindle; Paul Harvey, "Butch O'Hare (his father Artful Eddie)," Paul Harvey Archives, last updated February 19, 2019, http://www.paulharveyarchives.com/trots/b/.

Vertical Performance
Leadership & Management Consulting

Vertical Performance Enterprises is a U.S. veteran-owned leadership and management consulting company specializing in executive leadership development and organizational performance improvement. We work with leaders in mission-critical industries to help take their teams to the next level through the application of proven leadership principles and performance improvement fundamentals that have consistently produced winning results in complex, uncertain, and dynamic operating environments. *Our mission is to help leaders inspire their teams to change their world.*

OUR **APPROACH** CONCENTRATES
ON THREE KEY QUESTIONS:

1. **STRATEGY**
What do you want to achieve, and why?

2. **CHANGE MANAGEMENT**
What changes will you need to make to get there?

3. **LEADERSHIP DEVELOPMENT**
How will you develop leaders who can implement these changes, sustain progress toward your goal, and manage risk along the way?

CORE SERVICES INCLUDE:

▶ **Customized group leadership training**

▶ **Senior leadership team development**

▶ **One-on-one leadership coaching**

To learn more about how Vertical Performance can help take your team to the next level, contact us at **www.verticalperformance.us.**

CPSIA information can be obtained
at www.ICGtesting.com
Printed in the USA
BVHW060825150921
616730BV00023B/235/J

9 781954 020092